PSYCHIC TAROT

Written by Craig Junjulas

**Illustrated with the
AQUARIAN TAROT DECK**

by David Palladini

U.S. GAMES SYSTEMS, INC.
Publishers • Stamford, CT 06902 USA

COPYRIGHT© 1985, 2023 Craig Junjulas

All rights reserved. The illustrations, cover design, and contents are protected by copyright. No part of this book may be reproduced in any graphic, electronic or mechanical form including photocopying, recording, taping or by any information storage retrieval system without permission in writing from the publisher, except by a reviewer who wishes to quote brief passages in connection with a review for inclusion in a print publication or online platform.

Library of Congress Cataloging in Publication Data

Junjulas, Craig, 1952–
Psychic Tarot.

Bibliography: p.120
1. Tarot   2. Psychical research.   3. Occult sciences.
I. Title.

10 9 8 7 6 5 4 3 2

Made in China

Published by
U.S. GAMES SYSTEMS, INC.
179 Ludlow Street • Stamford, CT 06902 USA
www.usgamesinc.com

TABLE OF CONTENTS

PREFACE 7

CHAPTER ONE

THE TAROT DECK... 10

CHAPTER TWO

DEVELOPING PSYCHIC ABILITIES 25
    Understanding Our Triune Consciousness 29
    Energy and the Human Aura 33
    Chakras: Psychic Energy Centers of the
        Human Body 37
    Clearing the Mind with Meditation...................... 44
    Preparing for Psychic Readings 46
    Avoiding Common Problems on the Path 53
    Technique for Self-healing................................... 55

CHAPTER THREE

PSYCHIC RECEPTION 56
   Learning To Hear Clearly 57
   Learning To See Clearly 60
   Using the Other Senses 63
   Other Ways to Receive Psychic Information 66

CHAPTER FOUR

THE MAJOR ARCANA AS A SPIRITUAL JOURNEY .. 70

CHAPTER FIVE

THE MAJOR ARCANA 76

CHAPTER SIX

THE MINOR ARCANA 109
   The Rods 109
   The Swords 118
   The Cups 127
   The Pentacles 136

CHAPTER SEVEN

INTUITION AND THE TAROT 146
   Six of Pentacles 149
   The Tower 151

Four of Swords 153
A Potpourri of Intuitions 155

CHAPTER EIGHT

PERFORMING PSYCHIC TAROT READINGS 159

The Yes/No Spread 162
The Ancient Celtic Cross Spread 164
The Astrological Spread 173
Circular Spread for Yearly Forecast 175

APPENDIX 176

Numerological Correlation to the Tarot 176
Astrological Correlation to the Major Arcana 179
Chart: Trends in the Tarot Cards 183

BIBLIOGRAPHY 186

ABOUT THE AUTHOR 188

NOTES: Personal Interpretations & Intuitions 189

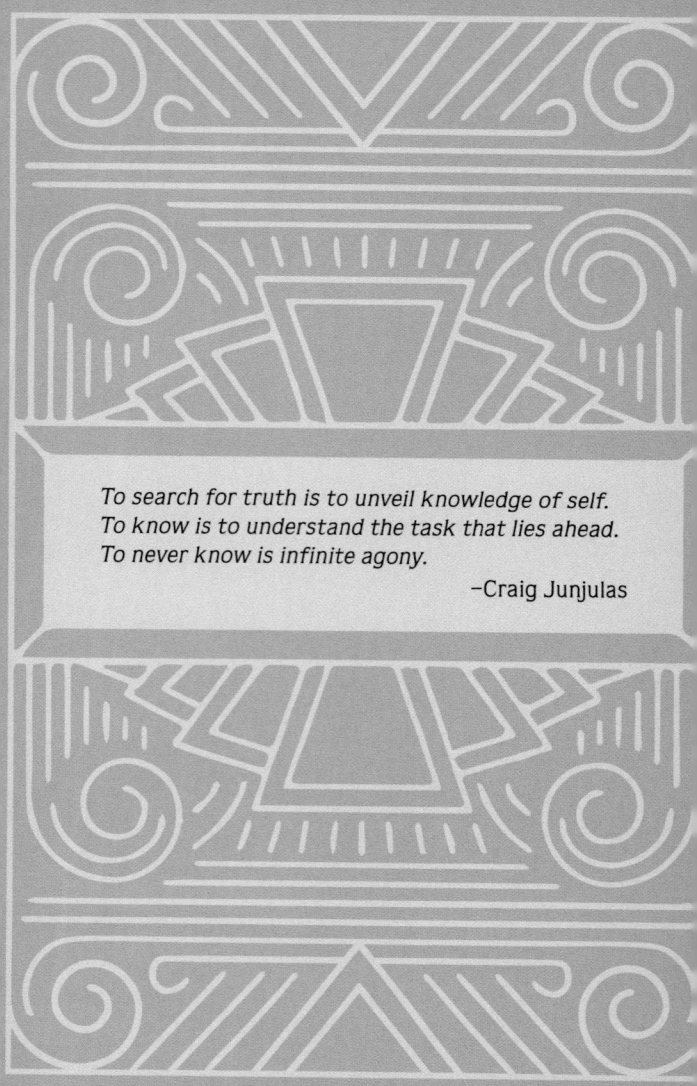

*To search for truth is to unveil knowledge of self.
To know is to understand the task that lies ahead.
To never know is infinite agony.*

—Craig Junjulas

PREFACE

The purpose of this book is to create a bridge between two subjects that are dear to me: psychic development and the Tarot. This bridge can be crossed from either direction. If you are investigating or working with Tarot cards, you can cross comfortably into the realm of psychic development. If you have been interested or involved in psychic development, you will be able to explore the fascinating world of the Tarot.

As an instructor of personal and psychic development, I have enjoyed introducing people to many benefits of opening up to this exciting subject. I try to reduce the esoteric teachings to simple terms and relate the teachings to everyday experience. I believe that everyone has psychic abilities and can develop them easily and safely by using common sense and sincerity.

I also believe that the Tarot cards can lead the student through soul development in an exciting and practical way. The cards contain the esoteric wisdom that is revealed through pictures and related to everyday experiences. Sincere use of the Tarot cards in psychic readings aids both the reader and the seeker to grow and be healed as they work together. I recommend their use for students who are training to be aura readers and healers because the cards can communicate important information about a seeker that the reader may not see by looking directly at a person's energy. I also teach the Tarot cards as a meditative tool for receiving spiritual insight and wisdom.

I recommend the Aquarian Tarot deck because I feel that David Palladini was inspired when he created the artwork for this deck. He has blended the ancient symbols with modern images and colors that speak directly to the spirits heralding the Aquarian Age. This particular deck has a tremendous emotional impact on the user and seems to awaken the desire to help other souls who are searching for the meaning of life at this time.

This book is written with both the beginning student and the advanced practitioner in mind. Beginning readers are often confused by the variations in meanings they read for each card and become frustrated when they try to use these meanings in actual reading situations. Each author has his, or her, own interpretation of the meanings and symbology for each Tarot card because the cards interact with each person's subconscious mind. Understanding this process will help the beginning student use the various interpretations as a help, rather than a hindrance.

I have blended traditional and modern meanings together, along with my own insights, and presented them in levels that offer choices without confusion. You will be familiarizing yourself with the basic interpretations of the cards, and scoring these meanings in your subconscious mind as you study. By learning the Tarot while working with psychic development, you will be assisted by the techniques that teach you to trust psychic impressions that come to you from your own subconscious when needed. Acceptance of these intuitive insights removes the mental pressure and confusion that usually result from trying to remember and apply the meanings that you read.

The advanced student or practitioner will enjoy the opportunity for expansion and growth offered by the practical psychic development techniques which are incorporated into this system. The additional inspiration and healing energy that is provided by this system should enable you to help others successfully.

I hope the following pages inspire you and gently awaken your psychic abilities as you open your mind and heart to these teachings. May the light that is within you shine out on all humanity and reflect the love, wisdom and power of your higher self as you work with *Psychic Tarot*.

C. J.

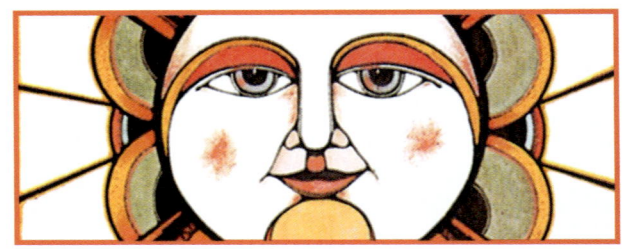

CHAPTER ONE
THE TAROT DECK

The Tarot is a complete and powerful system of communication in picture form. It is an inspired arrangement of images, symbols, words and numbers that portray the general meaning of the cards as well as house the esoteric symbols. The Tarot cards deal with every facet of human existence and teach us about the nonphysical aspects of our universe. They make available to us a universal wisdom, which can be instrumental in awakening our psychic senses and in the transmission of divinatory messages.

The wisdom embodied in the cards occurs on many levels. As you develop and are ready to understand a deeper level of knowledge, the cards will seem to speak in a new way. You may look at a familiar card and be surprised by your new perception. Sometimes cards almost seem alive in their ability to give you timely information and insight equivalent to your need and depth of understanding.

The origin of the Tarot is a mystery, and its history only dimly known, though many speculative theories about it have been publicized. Before the rise of European kings and queens and the traveling bands of Romani people who were said to have brought the Tarot to Europe, the Tarot's history is a void. Is the Tarot a teaching system brought from the ancient civilization of Atlantis? Did the great teachers from that continent preserve and carry with them these seeds of wisdom to plant in the new epoch? Were the halls of the initiatory chamber of the great pyramid of Egypt lined with the 22 pictures of the Major Arcana to carry on the traditional teachings from antediluvian times? These questions can be answered only speculatively at the present time, but they add to the mystery and the appeal of the Tarot.

The various Tarot decks created over the past few centuries gave rise to many artistic interpretations. Each artist drew from the ancient system to illustrate a newly styled deck. Many of the drawings and paintings were done by artists who worked according to the specifications of a sponsor. Kings and queens, occultists, and independent publishers sponsored, and therefore influenced, the creation of new Tarot decks. However varied the artistic interpretations of the Tarot, the basic teachings were woven into each deck.

The Aquarian Tarot, which illustrates this book, was chosen because of its emotional and spiritual impact and its relevancy to the present time period. The deck blends ancient symbolism and art deco design elements within a framework and background of medieval artistry.

The Tarot deck contains 78 cards and is divided into two sections: the Major Arcana and the Minor Arcana (*arcana* is Latin for "secrets"). The Major Arcana has 22 cards and represents the cosmic forces that affect human and spiritual development. The Minor Arcana has 56 cards that portray the myriad of human conditions and life situations. Together, they express the interactions between the spiritual world and temporal human beings on their journey through time on Earth.

THE MAJOR ARCANA

The cards of the Major Arcana are titled, and are numbered from zero to 21 with Roman numerals. They can be subdivided into three distinct groups of seven cards each, called septenaries, with the zero card, titled the Fool, as a separate entity. Cards numbered I through VII reveal the inner nature of man, his virtues, needs, and vices. Cards VIII through XIV show the forces placed upon him from his environment. Cards XV through XXI, the third septenary, represent the cosmic influences upon him. The Fool card has the designation of zero and has been the subject of much debate as to whether it belongs at the beginning or the end of the Major Arcana.

The Fool is related to all cards in the Major Arcana and is both the beginning and the end, the alpha and omega, the neophyte and the mystical master. It is the card that connects all of the cards in the Major Arcana together in the spiritual journey taken.

THE MINOR ARCANA

The Minor Arcana contains 56 cards divided into four distinct suits: Rods, Swords, Cups, and Pentacles. Each suit has 14 cards: ten numbered cards and four court cards. The Ace through Ten of each suit represents the ideas and situations of earthly existence. The four court cards—Page, Knight, Queen, and King—can characterize people and their particular personality traits, or describe a human situation. The suits of the Minor Arcana illustrate the four planes of the earth and the way we deal with life situations.

The **Suit of Rods** represents the spiritual plane and the application of spiritual laws to daily life. The suit also represents our desire to attain new heights in our spiritual development and understanding. It teaches us about our relationship to cosmic energies by illustrating the need for us to accept our roots in nature and our continuous branching upward and outward to absorb the life-giving energy of the sun. The message contained within this suit is that the alignment of our life direction with spiritual principles provides for successful enterprises, greatness, honor and acclaim.

The **Suit of Swords** represents the mental plane and our thought processes. It describes how we handle difficulties in our spiritual evolution, and the many forms of incorrect thinking that seem to weaken and enslave the human being. Many of the figures in this suit have downcast, hidden, or covered eyes, which attest to their reluctance to allow others to see their mental confusion or pain, or their inability to see their own problems clearly. Activity, hostility, strife, animosity, and misfortune are the essence of the teaching methods conveyed by the swords. They relate to analytical thinking, politics, warfare, and understanding creative ideas and taking action to effect a change.

The **Suit of Cups** illustrates the emotional plane and our internal reactions to life situations. It shows us how to perceive and accept the human emotions as an internal system of reactions and signals that teach us how to better interact with each other and our environment. It reminds us of the spark of divinity in each human heart, and of the gift of human feelings as a source of intimate communication. It also teaches us about the need to spend time and effort cleaning and polishing the human vessel that contains the soul.

The **Suit of Pentacles** stands for the physical plane and our material concerns. It describes the myriad conditions of human survival and accomplishment on the physical level. It teaches us how to perceive everyday experiences in relation to the total view of humanistic development. The pentacles relate to physical laws, measurable phenomena, and the tangible things in our lives. They also symbolize the physical manifestation of creative ideas and the rewards that follow the correct application of these ideas in daily life.

Though both the Major and Minor sections of the Tarot deck can be used separately for readings, the broadest type of understanding will come only by seeing the whole that is made of the parts. By using the complete deck, the reader can provide helpful information about the seeker's life situation through the Minor Arcana and describe the cosmic forces affecting it as revealed through the Major Arcana.

CONSIDER THE TAROT A MAP

A good way to study and feel comfortable with the Tarot deck is to try to see an overview of the whole system and its main divisions as if you were studying a map of a country before embarking on a cross-country trip. This view allows the driver to see the main routes without confusing details.

The next step would be to study a small group of cards at a time, such as the court cards of a suit, to become familiar with a specific section of the deck. This would correspond to tracing a route on a state map. This progressive fine-tuning would continue until each card has been studied independently, which is analogous to working from a local map to determine the best sights to see and places to stay.

When students feel overloaded and confused, they can either go back to an overview of the whole system or choose a single card on which to meditate. After a while they can return to the point at which they left off, and begin again with a fresh mind and a relaxed body.

Time, effort, and dedicated studies have made masters out of apprentices in many fields. As with other worthwhile fields of endeavor, the more time the student invests, the greater the potential for accomplishment.

PERSONAL VERSUS DEFINED MEANINGS

Some teachers of the Tarot instruct their students to look at, react to and write down their personal interpretations for each card. Other teachers have their students work from the defined meanings (also called "divinatory meanings") for each card as the sole source of interpretation. In between these two approaches are many methods that blend textbook definitions and instructor's meanings with the student's personal interpretations.

One problem inherent in using only personal interpretations is the limitation imposed by the student's life experiences and inability to see all aspects of humanity. The cards need to be allowed to express the full range of human behavior and warn of potentially harmful situations. The Tarot reader should be as capable of seeing the storm clouds that warn of rain, thunder, or lightning, as well as the clouds that suggest a silver lining.

Another problem associated with using only personal interpretations is the tendency of the experienced reader to project personal problems, hopes, and fears into the cards. For example, if the reader is experiencing problems with personal relationships, interpretation of all cards dealing with emotions and romantic feelings could become shaded by this difficulty. If the reader has unresolved conflicts with money and material possessions, the Suit of Pentacles could become a vehicle for this problem to be expressed. It is in the delicate learning stage that the traditional meanings of the cards can protect against such projection and guide the student toward the broader direction of psychic interpretation. On the other hand, if a person uses only textbook definitions in a Tarot reading, the information is limited by the written word, and does not allow the power of the deck to speak to the seeker. A psychic Tarot reader uses both.

DIVINATORY MEANINGS

The divinatory meanings of the Tarot cards vary among teachers and authors alike. Divinatory meanings, as given in the chapters on the Major Arcana and the Minor Arcana, are a collection of the generally accepted interpretations of the cards. They are provided as a teaching aid and as a guide to show the possible meanings attributed to each card. These definitions can be studied and stored in the student's long-term memory and edited and expanded upon as the student learns more about each card through personal use and meditation.

SYMBOLS

The symbols used in the Tarot deck are a form of universal language that survives temporary interpretation and usage. The symbols were formed in the collective unconscious of the human race and are part of the dream vocabulary of every man, woman and child, regardless of ethnic or cultural background. The sun, for example, has always stood for protecting and nurturing of the planet. It not only provides warmth and light, it is the very heart of the solar system. There may be some variation between the interpretation of the sun symbol of a man living in the desert and a man living in the arctic circle, but the life-giving nature of the sun remains intact.

Throughout the ages the sun symbol has adorned cave walls, temples, banners, and medallions as an expression of appreciation for it as a source of cosmic energy and life-giving light.

The symbols used throughout the Tarot deck also connect the viewer to the thoughts and emotions of the akashic records. The akashic records are the nonphysical chronicles of all events, thoughts, and emotions that have taken place in creation. Each symbol contains volumes of information that has been expressed about it and is stored in the energies of the universe. These nonphysical writings can be retrieved by focusing on a particular symbol and becoming receptive to the intuitive information that ensues. An example of the power and information of a simple symbol can be realized by focusing on the symbol for infinity, the horizontal eight above the head of the Magician in the Major Arcana. One could fill many notebooks by meditating on this sign and writing down intuitive information received from it.

WORDS

The title of each card, as well as the picture on it, is associated with a particular divinatory meaning and has a symbolic power of its own that can evoke images within a person. Consider the words themselves and what they suggest to you: Magician, Lovers, Hermit, Devil and Strength in the Major Arcana, for example. King, Queen or Knight in the Minor Arcana. Individual associations vary, of course, but the words connect to that powerful, deep subconscious vocabulary in each of us.

NUMBERS

Numbers also are an integral part of the Tarot deck. They not only designate the procession of the cards within a section but have a message all their own. Each number has an occult significance and an idea associated with it. The number one represents beginnings, therefore the Ace of each suit deals with the starting point of each suit's general message. The divinatory meanings of the numbered cards are based partly on numerological factors. A basic understanding of the field of numerology—the study and evaluation of numbers and their influence on human conditions—will benefit the serious student of Tarot (see Appendix, page 176).

For the psychic Tarot reader, numbers might suggest something in the seeker's life. An awareness of the numbers as they relate to the spread of the cards can add to the depth of a reading. In other words, allow all aspects of the cards to speak to you—the pictures, words and numbers.

PATTERNS AND SHAPES

The patterns and shapes in the Tarot cards, particularly in the Aquarian Tarot deck, which is a rich landscape of geometric shapes, can also trigger the creative imagination of the viewer. The empty spaces themselves can be used as blank screens on which to receive psychic information about the seeker in the form of images.

Psychic readers have used tools like tea leaves as a physical mechanism to bring out a message from the subconscious. The reader sees visions unfold through the interaction of the lines and shapes of the wet tea leaves as they form a pattern on the bottom of the cup. As a developmental technique the student can also stare at clouds in the sky and observe the images received while concentrating on a specific situation or person. Or, another way to deepen sensitivity to patterns and shapes is to use the inkblot test cards while concentrating on a friend and writing down the interpretations for them.

PERSONAL ENERGY AND THE CARDS

The deck that you use can be personally energized by your aura. Whenever you work with the cards you bathe them in the energy of your aura and record into the cards the pattern of your feelings, thoughts, and aspirations. If you are connected to the energy of your higher consciousness, your nonphysical guides, and spiritual love, wisdom, and power, your Tarot deck can become a part of that connection and symbolize it. This is one reason for sleeping with a new Tarot deck under your pillow; the spiritual energies of the higher realms flow through your body and into the cards during sleep.

Another reason for placing a new deck under your pillow is to create an energy link between your aura and the cards. The information contained in the Tarot deck filters into your subconscious mind as you sleep, while your aura programs the cards with its particular frequencies.

The Tarot cards are an extension of your subconscious communication system. They speak to you by stimulating inner thoughts, feelings, and images that provide a deeper understanding of yourself and life. Mastery of the Tarot gently awakens your psychic abilities and guides you to higher personal and spiritual development. It also teaches you the greater purposes of divination and its application for helping others in need of assistance.

SPREADS

The mixing and laying out of Tarot cards in a particular pattern, for the purpose of divination, is called a spread. The cards are turned face up and interpreted according to the placement within the spread and in relation to each other. Each position is defined according to its area of influence on the seeker and provides a sense of timing of events and influences. These influences are related to one another, hence the meaning of a card located in a position relating to the past will affect the interpretation of a card placed in a future position.

One spread that is very popular is the Ancient Celtic Cross. This spread, which will be described later in more detail, has a broad scope, yet can answer specific questions asked by a seeker. Each placement of the ten cards used in this layout has a particular message to impart. These ten positions cover a broad range of influences on the seeker: from general influences, to the effect of the environment, to the eventual outcome of the matter being investigated. It covers the internal and external influences and gives perspectives on the past, present and future situations.

When a card is reversed within the context of a spread it can change the meaning of the card. Some cards are given opposite definitions when reversed, some change less drastically, and a few remain unchanged. The interpretation depends not only on the cards that are upside down, but on the other cards surrounding it.

If a card is defined as having an opposite meaning when reversed, yet is surrounded by other cards that support the upright definition, it may mean something in between the two. For example, if the Two of Cups is reversed and is influenced by many cards showing love and happiness, instead of describing false love and separation, it may be warning of the need for more friendship and cooperation at the beginning of a love relationship. By using psychic receptivity supported by the divinatory meanings stored in the subconscious, the psychic Tarot reader will be able to sense the story being told by the spread and know intuitively how to interpret the cards.

A MUTUAL POINT OF FOCUS

During a psychic Tarot reading the cards become a mutual point of focus. The reader and the seeker both have something to look at while they talk about personal matters pertaining to the seeker's soul and life situation. With the cards as a buffer, the seeker is more accepting of information received, as if the cards are responsible for the information revealed and the psychic reader is simply an interpreter.

CONCLUSION

The combination of a study of psychic development techniques with the study and practice of Tarot reading connects two very exciting systems together that support and fuel each other. As in all systems from philosophies to atomic power, it is our choice how to use the system. Psychic Tarot reading can be used to its highest capacity to do good works and bring joy, or it can be misused, or knowingly abused. The Magician, when reversed, for example, becomes undignified and represents the misuse and abuse of power, which is the avoidance of truth combined with the application of power for personal gain, often at the expense of others.

The interaction between your psychic self and mind and the Tarot cards will determine the quality of learning you will experience. The interaction between yourself and other people will determine how you use what you learn. But it will be your good intentions, your clear and creative thinking and positive actions that will make your study of these systems a heart-warming, enlightening, and spiritually rewarding journey.

CHAPTER TWO
DEVELOPING PSYCHIC ABILITIES

Psychic ability is a natural human talent, more commonly referred to as intuition. It is a creative talent that can be developed and refined through study and practice. If you consider psychic ability in line with other creative talents, you will not feel separated from it, or believe that it is a special "power" that only a few select individuals are blessed with.

Many scientific breakthroughs and inventions are the result of creative, or intuitive, flashes of inspiration. Scientists often find the solution to their scientific problems, after extensive research and trials, through visions or dreams. The modern sewing machine, for example, was created when the inventor remembered a dream about natives chasing him with spears that had eyes on the spear heads. When the inventor creatively applied what he learned through his dream, that is to thread the needle through the point instead of the back, the sewing machine was born.

Psychic ability, simply put, is the creative application of human intuition. It is the tapping of the subconscious part of the mind and allowing it to become a channel for clearer understanding and higher knowledge. Working psychically means to allow information to unfold while you are in a state of receptivity, as opposed to consciously working out or constructing your ideas. You open your intuitive system, tune into a particular situation, and become conscious of the understanding it provides.

A modern definition of a psychic* describes a person who is apparently sensitive to nonphysical or supernatural forces and influences and marked by extraordinary or mysterious sensitivity, perception, or understanding. If you eliminate the words "apparently," "extraordinary," and "mysterious," you are left with a human being who is sensitive to energy, and is perceptive and understanding. These traits can be awakened and developed in you, or anyone else who is willing to work with them.

Some people will have more of a capacity to develop psychic abilities than others, just as it is with other talents. Just because individuals do not have extraordinary musical talent it should not prevent them from learning to play an instrument, or possibly making a living as entertainers. It only means that hard work and practice are necessary for the achievement of realistic goals.

In psychic awareness classes almost all of the students are pleasantly surprised with their natural psychic abilities in reading objects for the first time. They hold

---

*Webster's 11th New Collegiate Dictionary
©2021 by Merriam Webster Inc., Springfield, MA

sealed envelopes that contain objects brought in by their fellow students and find themselves able to tune into the characteristics and life events of the owner of the object (see Psychometry, page 66). They go home realizing psychic ability is an inherent human ability that is available to them.

Professional psychic readers describe their work as *channeling*, the reception of messages from an outside (nonphysical) source and the transference of this energy and information to assist another person. The process is similar to the function of a stereo system; the receiver picks up signals that are broadcast through the air and converts these energy signals back into the sounds that originated at the radio station.

Although professionals use various techniques to become more receptive, that is, to develop their psychic awareness, and describe the sources of their information in different words, the common thread is the reception from an outside source. Some claim to work with discarnate spirits who bring back messages from the spiritual plane. Others seek help from spirit guides, guardian angels, or other higher sources. Still other professional psychic readers describe the outside source as being a part of the subconscious or superconscious mind of the client or reader.

What lies within or beyond your own mind is for you to discover and interpret. As you investigate the psychic world you will realize that there is much beyond the physical world that is not understood. You will experience your own perception of the nonphysical and find terminology that suits your personal need for expression.

If you have a strong science background, you might investigate the nonphysical from an energy standpoint and reach out into greater consciousness from there. If your background is in psychology, your initial approach may be from personal consciousness and broaden into the areas of energy and spirit consciousness. If you have a strong religious foundation, you can build upon it to reach out into the nonphysical realms through spiritual research. It is important to understand that it is up to you to decide what to believe and how to go about practicing your beliefs. Other people, including teachers and authors, may share their own findings and conclusions with you, but you are the one who must decide ultimately what to discard and what to embrace. Psychic awareness is a personal system of opening and discovery.

UNDERSTANDING OUR TRIUNE CONSCIOUSNESS

Consciousness is energy that has a state of awareness: qualities of realization, perception and knowledge. Consciousness is energy that has cohesiveness, in that it is held together as a unity by its sense of self-identity and by its sense of purpose as a continuously evolving state of awareness. It also has the ability to direct itself into new areas of learning and can discern, evaluate and retain information. It can direct its course of action, through desire and willpower, to expand its awareness.

Human consciousness can be divided into three sections: the subconscious, conscious and superconscious mind. It may also be named: body, mind and spirit or psychic self, mental self and higher self. It is the integration and harmonizing of these three aspects of self that denote a healthy and balanced individual. A great deal of the joy and excitement of practical development comes from getting in touch with, and accepting, one's inner nature, and growing as a total person. Further, it is the joyous union and the harmonious working together of the triune consciousness that marks a high caliber psychic Tarot reader.

THE SUBCONSCIOUS MIND

The subconscious is the part of mind that maintains the automatic systems of the body, such as the respiration, heartbeat, and biochemistry. This area of mind also learns to control and direct the physical body in complex situations. When you first learn to drive a car, you are

programming your subconscious mind to operate the controls while you consciously perform the functions. After a while you end up letting your body press pedals, shift gears, and turn the wheel while your conscious mind takes in the scenery, solves a business prob-
lem, or makes decisions about other driving tasks, such as finding a particular address as you drive.

This "body consciousness" receives information simultaneously through the five senses and interprets and relays this information to the conscious mind. Another function of the subconscious mind is to store and cross-reference memories. The body also communicates to the mind through a system of energy signals called emotions and intuitive impressions. It is this last function, along with its ability to perceive the world in a way that is beyond the five senses, that gives the subconscious mind the label of "psychic self."

THE CONSCIOUS MIND

The conscious mind is the thinking part that processes the words you are reading and evaluates the information in a logical way. In general conversations it is the conscious mind that is referred to when one describes one's "self," though the conscious and subconscious are aspects of the same mind. To clarify this the psychology textbooks use an iceberg as a model to illustrate the conscious/subconscious continuum: the part of the iceberg above the water line is the conscious part, the larger portion that remains hidden beneath the water the subconscious.

The conscious and subconscious work together. For example, in the act of reading a book the two work together to process and evaluate the author's ideas and conclusions. The body collects the printed symbols on the page and turns them into words that are heard inside the ears. As the conscious mind listens to the words, it "thinks" about the concepts being presented. During this process the information is continuously passed through subconscious levels to connect with previously stored information. This inner working can be felt as a flow of energy between the solar plexus and the head. The information that is both logical and feels right is accepted as learning. The more open a person is to the subconscious processing, the greater the chances for new and exciting insights, and a deeper understanding of many subjects.

THE SUPERCONSCIOUS MIND

The superconscious mind, or "spirit self," is the great reservoir of wisdom that is available to those who reach out beyond the limitations of the conscious mind. The wisdom contained in the superconscious mind is the accumulation and integration of the experiences gathered from one's countless reincarnations. This aspect of mind is also called the "higher self" because it is considered to be the part of human consciousness that exists eternally in a higher level of reality.

> Reincarnation is the gathering together of specific areas of this spirit consciousness and its repeated descent into physical lifetimes. The portion that is invested into a human lifetime is sometimes referred to as the "soul," which for the purpose of this discussion is the subconscious and conscious mind combined. The major portion that remains behind, and exists eternally in a higher level of reality, is the "higher self."

IN PSYCHIC TAROT READINGS

In psychic Tarot readings the subconscious, or the "psychic self" mentioned before, is responsible for sensing and converting energy patterns into psychic information and is the direct link to superconsciousness and spiritual guides. The conscious mind is responsible for the logical and professional presentation of this information and for the delivery of healing energy.

A helpful analogy is to compare the conscious mind to a well; the subconscious to the water in the well; and the superconscious, or higher self, to the constant supply of water flowing to the well from the comparatively vast water table. If there are muddy waters, or psychological blocks in the reader's subconscious, the quality and quantity of psychic information received will be unreliable and psychic reception unclear. Introspection and self-healing are important to the reader because the helpfulness of a Tarot reading depends on the openness and clarity of this system.

ENERGY AND THE HUMAN AURA

Developing your psychic ability will mean increasing your sensitivity to nonphysical forces, paying more attention not only to spiritual forces, thoughts and emotions, but also to subtle energy vibrations.

All of life is composed of energy. The stars, the planets, and all things that make up the universe are actually energy in different forms and states of vibration. The three forms of matter—solids, liquids, and gases—are made up of small particles called atoms. Between 1803 and 1808, an English chemist named John Dalton revived the ancient Greek belief (ca. 500 BC) that all matter was composed of basic units called atoms.

All atoms have the same internal structure. They are made up of even smaller particles called protons, neutrons and electrons. The only difference between an atom of lead and an atom of oxygen is the number of these subatomic particles of energy. In the early 1900s scientists discovered that all forms of energy, which include subatomic particles, could be divided into even smaller units called quanta. A quantum is an individual bundle or packet of energy that can act either as a particle or a wave.

Einstein defined the relationship between matter and energy with his famous equation $E = mc^2$; that is, energy is equal to mass (or matter) accelerated to the speed of light squared. This equation seems to say matter is a "densification" of energy.

Energy is manifested in many ways; heat, light and electricity are forms of energy. The electromagnetic spectrum is used to demonstrate the continuity of energy by showing the measurement of the length and frequency of energy. The only difference between radio waves, visible light and gamma rays is the length of the energy wave, and how frequently it occurs.

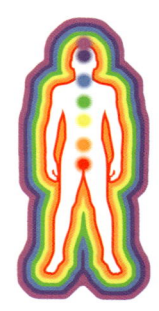

Of these, radio waves have the longest wavelength and the lowest frequency. Radio waves used for commercial broadcasting are many meters long and have a frequency ranging from 550 to 1,600 kilohertz (kHz). The numbers on radio dials stand for thousands of cycles per second. Radio waves greater than 1,600,000 cycles per second and shorter in length are called shortwaves.

Visible light is this same energy at shorter wavelengths (around one millionth of a meter long) and at higher frequency. Gamma rays are less than one ten-billionth of a meter long and have a frequency greater than 1,000,000,000,000,000 cycles per second.

The human body is composed of chemicals that are combinations of atoms. Atoms, in turn, are configurations of particles of energy. The energy field around the human body, called the human aura, is a continuation of the physical body in less dense patterns. The energy of the aura has a higher frequency of vibration as it exists farther out from the physical body. The common names given to the levels of energy, in order of increasing vibra-

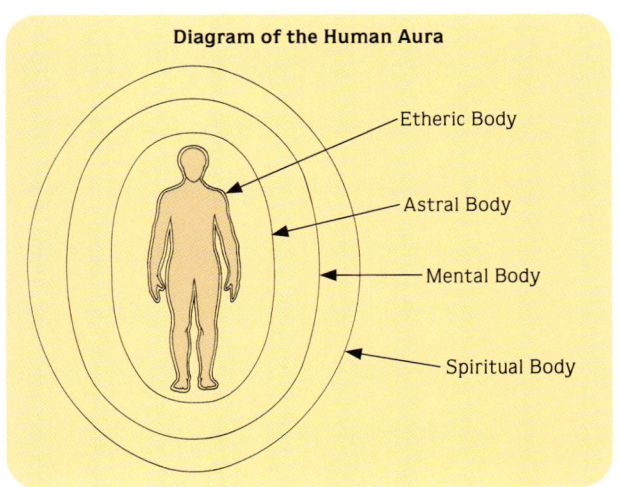

tion, are: the etheric, the astral, the mental and spiritual bodies. Some teaching systems describe other levels, or use different names, but the concepts are similar.

THE ETHERIC BODY

The energy body that permeates and closely surrounds the physical body is called the etheric body. It appears as an inch or two of brightly glowing, yellow light, conforming to the shape of the physical body.

The etheric body is also called the health body. It contains the energy blueprint of the physical body's state of harmony and well-being. The esoteric description of disease incorporates the concepts of mind/body dis-ease, or uneasiness, resulting in disturbance of the aura field. In health readings this energy is studied for signs of blockage of energy flow. Abnormal etheric energy patterns can be psychically perceived before the physical body shows signs of any problem.

THE ASTRAL BODY

The astral body is the multicolored, ovate energy that extends about a foot or two beyond the etheric body. The astral body, also called the emotional body, is the area of the aura where feelings are recorded and displayed as energy patterns. This energy is neon-like and in a constant state of flux as it expresses the emotional changes of a person from moment to moment.

THE MENTAL BODY

Beyond the astral body is the mental body, the energy zone affected by our thoughts. Mental processes are imprinted and stored in this band of energy. If the mental body is afflicted with negative thought patterns, it can be healed in a psychic reading when the thought patterns are changed to a more positive form.

THE SPIRITUAL BODY

The remaining energy in the human aura is called the spiritual body. The further away from the physical body the energy is, the higher the vibration and the softer the colors. Because of its distance from the physical body and the consciousness within it, this energy is most easily influenced by outside sources. Thus, one technique frequently used for psychic protection is to imagine a protective shield of radiant white light at the outermost edge of the aura, that part of the spiritual body that interfaces with the outer world and is most vulnerable to it.

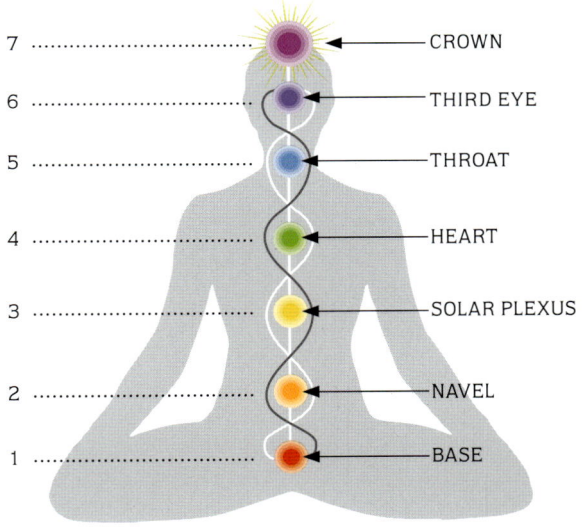

Diagram of the Seven Chakras

CHAKRAS: PSYCHIC ENERGY CENTERS OF THE HUMAN BODY

Within these energy bodies are centers of vortexing energy that connect them together and allow the flow of energy to pass between them. These energy centers are called *chakras*, which is the Sanskrit word for "wheels" or "lotuses" used in yoga. In psychic work the main function of the chakras is to convert energy into information. There are seven major psychic energy centers, or chakras, located along the spinal column. Each chakra is associated with an endocrine gland and labeled according to the area of the body in which it is located. The common names, in ascending order from the bottom of the spine, are 1) Base; 2) Navel; 3) Solar Plexus; 4) Heart; 5) Throat; 6) Third Eye; and 7) Crown. These are the points along the physical body where the aura bodies connect and join the spinal column.

1. THE BASE CHAKRA

The base chakra is the most physical and is referred to as the sexual center. If the reader focuses on this chakra in a reading, psychic impressions relating to the physical reality of the seeker can rise up the spine and be expressed. The resulting information can sometimes include detailed descriptions of cars, houses, people and other physical situations in the seeker's life.

In many esoteric training programs, energy is directed into this chakra and redirected up to the crown to bring about spiritual enlightenment. In yoga teachings this process is called "raising the kundalini." The practice of celibacy is also associated with the transformation of sexual/physical energy into spiritual energy. The caduceus, the symbol of the medical profession, portrays this esoteric process of spiritual enlightenment. Two snakes wind down through the chakras, touch the base, and the center spinal shaft carries the transformed energy to the winged ball at the top. The ball represents the crown chakra, and the wings dramatize the conversion of the energy to spirituality.

2. THE NAVEL CHAKRA

The navel chakra, the center for sensual energy, is known as the storehouse for "ki" energy in certain martial arts schools. Powerful energy from the earth and from one's own aura is drawn up through the base of the spine. This energy is collected and concentrated in the navel chakra, then released through the hands or other parts of the body, and returned to the earth.

3. THE SOLAR PLEXUS

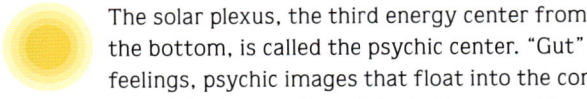
The solar plexus, the third energy center from the bottom, is called the psychic center. "Gut" feelings, psychic images that float into the conscious mind, and the inner voice originate from or at least pass through this chakra. It is sometimes used as a point of focus for the subconscious mind.

Intense energy responses to life situations as well as internal responses are felt in the solar plexus. It reacts to both seen and unseen conditions that are potentially threatening by tightening, quivering, or actively responding in some other manner. Unresolved internal conflicts leave a knotted feeling here, while peaceful states of mind leave a warm glowing gut feeling. Happiness and excitement create a sensation of an upward energy movement, also one of the signals for "yes" from the psychic self. Nervous anticipation is described as "butterflies in the stomach." The psychic gut response for "no" and the stronger response of anger register as a tightening and sinking feeling in this area.

4. THE HEART CHAKRA

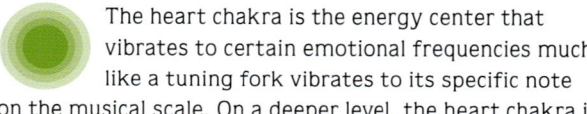

The heart chakra is the energy center that vibrates to certain emotional frequencies much like a tuning fork vibrates to its specific note on the musical scale. On a deeper level, the heart chakra is the spiritual temple for the spark of divinity that is within everyone, sometimes called the "Christ Consciousness," the "I AM" or the spiritual self.

The heart center, located halfway between the base and the crown, is the fourth chakra out of seven. Because the lower three chakras are the realm of the body (subconscious), and the upper three the realm of the "thinking" mind (conscious), the heart is the mediator between the two. It is the place your mind enters to achieve the peaceful state called "centering."

5. THE THROAT CHAKRA

The throat chakra is the communicating center. When people express their thoughts through the spoken word, the vibrations are converted into sound waves that convey the total message, that is, the feelings as well as the words. Even subconscious thought patterns pass out through the throat chakra, sometimes as embarrassing slips of the tongue known as "Freudian slips."

When people consciously tell a lie or deny their true feelings, their throat chakra is affected as a tightening or dryness in the throat or a feeling of energy trying to break through a barrier and out through the voice. In some cases, energy flow from the gut and heart is so intense the eyes tear. Most people can sense what another is really feeling even if the words are opposite, or unsaid.

In psychic Tarot readings, both spoken and unspoken feelings of hope and spiritual guidance should be allowed to flow freely from the reader's throat chakra. Higher inspiration sometimes manifests itself in eloquent spontaneous analogies.

6. THE THIRD EYE

The sixth chakra is called the third eye. This chakra includes the forehead, the physical eyes, the nose, and the temples in its energy vortex. It is symbolized by a small circle above the bridge of the nose, representing the center of the chakra. It is the area of visual perception as well as the projection center for thought waves and is often considered the focal point of the *sixth sense*. When Tarot readers close their eyes and relax into this chakra, they see psychic information as internal images. In the Tarot cards, many characters have symbols on this part of the body, drawing the reader's attention to this chakra and to the implications of the symbol in the context of the seeker's life situation.

7. THE CROWN CHAKRA

The seventh chakra is the crown, the center that has the highest vibrational rate of all the chakras; the place where spiritual energy interacts with the physical body. The crown chakra can be divided into five working sections to help the mind direct specific energies through this active area of the aura.

The top of the crown chakra is a channel for energy from the upper aura to flow into the spinal column.

When this energy, sometimes called "chi" or "ki," is drawn into the body, it raises the vibrational rate of all the chakras. A harmonious flow of energy throughout the aura can be created by visualizing drawing in the aura energy while at the same time directing the old, unused energy out through the feet into the earth. This "refueling process" increases the efficiency of the chakras for converting energy into psychic information in a Tarot reading.

One side of the crown chakra draws healing energy into the spinal column while the opposite side releases unwanted energy completely free of the aura. Working with these two areas of the crown chakra would be particularly useful for a psychic Tarot reader. Instead of absorbing the problems (unwanted, or negative energy) of the seeker, as can happen, the reader receives them and allows them to pass through and out this area of the chakra.

The area around the ears is for clairaudience, or clear listening. One ear may favor listening to nonphysical vibrations, while the other favors listening to sound waves on the physical plane. An easy way to find out which ear is physically oriented is to pay attention to the ear dominantly used during a lengthy telephone conversation. When the phone is switched to the nonphysical ear, to rest the tired one, observe how it inevitably finds its way back to the physical side through a subconscious act.

The back of the neck is another channel through the crown chakra. When the chin rests on the chest, as it does in an attitude of prayer, the vertebra at the base of the skull becomes the top of the antenna. Spiritual energy then flows directly from the spine to the heart and lower chakras without passing through the sometime chaotic processes of the mind. The only frequency of energy that passes through this portal is the spiritual energy of your higher self (superconsciousness) and the love, wisdom, and power of the highest consciousness; the connection made when someone requests spiritual guidance through prayer.

CHAKRAS AND THE TAROT CARDS

Knowledge of the chakras can be applied to the imagery of the Tarot cards. Note the location of ornaments, such as the jewel over the third eye chakra of the King of Rods,

which emphasizes his spiritual insight as part of his authority and strength. In contrast, the inverted star over the Devil's third eye chakra suggests the perversion of the chakra's spiritual function. The material aspect of life, symbolized by the pentacles, seems to block the heart and crown chakra of the young man in the Four of Pentacles. The jewel on the throat chakra of the overweight man on the Nine of Cups might be a warning of the dangers of overindulgence in food and drink. Pay attention to the chakras suggested on some of the Tarot cards and trust what comes to you as you meditate on them for specific seekers.

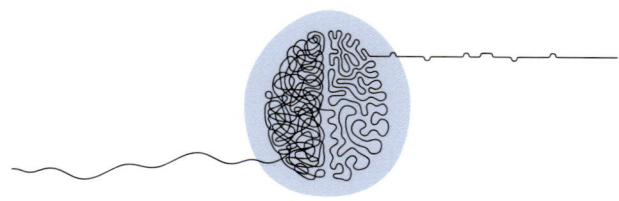

CLEARING THE MIND WITH MEDITATION

Meditation can be a helpful way to clear your mind for better results in your psychic development. Meditation begins with relaxing and becoming conscious of the internal thoughts, images, and feelings that flow through your mind naturally. Most of what you experience when you pay attention is a confusing chatter, unclear imagery, and swirling energy sensations all mixed together and moving at high speeds. Thoughts flow through your mind constantly. Throughout the day you are subject to thousands of internal visions and energy sensations. At night you experience this internal information as dreams.

You need to remove the tension within your mind and body to allow these impressions to flow through your mind while you are awake and aware; in essence, to train yourself to dream while you are awake. The combination of becoming aware of this internal process and reducing the disruptive energy patterns that tensions create will bring you to a deeper understanding of your own system of internal messages. This is important because you will be using these pictures, words and feelings to convey psychic information while using the Tarot cards. However, you need to differentiate between what is your own personal message and what is a valid psychic impression being shown to you through this system. In other words, you need to erase the blackboard before you draw the next lesson on it.

MEDITATION TECHNIQUE

Sit comfortably in a chair and take slow, deep breaths for a few minutes. As your body continues this rhythmic breathing naturally, begin to pay more attention to the pictures, words, and feelings that pass through your mind. After a few more minutes allow these images and thoughts to escape by acknowledging the messages they contain and then not paying any more attention to them, letting them go. Treat them as if they are unimportant and ignore them. Don't hold them inside your head by analyzing them, arguing with them, or becoming excited by them...simply let them go. After about five minutes, begin the second stage described below. Return to the first stage whenever disruptive thoughts or images occur.

    The second stage of this meditation involves focusing your mind on a repetitive symbol. Choose a simple word, like "love" or a mantra, such as "OM," as a focal point for your mind. Try to imagine large block letters of the word you have chosen against a star-filled background, like those showing the titles in movies. As you breathe in, see this image clearly in front of your closed eyes. Each time you exhale, visualize the word shooting off into space while you hear its sound (e.g., ooooooommmm, or whatever you choose) resonating inside your whole body. As the letters get smaller, the sound gets softer until you are left with a clear space again. Repeat this with each breath and allow yourself to drift into a peaceful meditative state.

This technique, practiced regularly—twenty minutes every day to a few times per week—will release your mind from everyday concerns and occupy it with a single thought or focus until it opens to a higher vibration. By consciously feeling the desire to attain a specific goal, such as knowing more about a particular subject or developing greater awareness of your own psychic abilities, you can direct the meditation instead of leaving it as an open experience.

PREPARING FOR PSYCHIC READINGS

The three developmental techniques provided in the following pages are designed to help the student relax and heighten psychic awareness; increase the flow and vibration of energy in the aura; and become connected to a higher source for protection and guidance. At first they can be practiced as a set of exercises that takes ten to twenty minutes. After the student becomes comfortable with the total process, the entire series can be condensed into a single exercise that can be performed in a few minutes.

RELAX AND HEIGHTEN PSYCHIC AWARENESS

To relax means to loosen, to make less compact. It involves the inactivation and lengthening of the muscle fibers of the body, accompanied by an expanded and dissociated state of mental consciousness. When deep relaxation techniques are used—whatever the technique—the person is sending a message to the body saying, "I am going to spend the following time in a comfortable and safe place where I do not need to be using my muscles." While the muscles are loosening, the person's mental consciousness is expanding and flowing into the whole body, from toes to head, filling this space. Nervous tension and anxiety are relieved and psychic receptivity is facilitated through the attainment of a state of physical and mental equilibrium.

RELAXATION TECHNIQUE

Sit comfortably in a chair with your head and body completely supported, or lie on a couch or bed, or exercise mat on the floor.

Inhale deeply, and slowly, through your nostrils. Hold your breath for a few seconds, then exhale through your mouth. As you rhythmically repeat this deep breathing, imagine the tension of the day escaping through your mouth with every breath.

Inhale and hold your breath as you tighten every muscle in your body. Feel the compression of your muscles, then exhale and let your muscles totally relax, so your body feels loose and limp, like a rag doll.

Return to the deep, rhythmic breathing, and imagine warm, soothing energy surrounding your feet, as if they were soaking in warm salt water. Feel the muscles loosening and lengthening and the nerves sending smooth, relaxing signals to every muscle fiber. Feel the blood flowing gently and smoothly up your legs, carrying this warming energy up your body.

As the warmth travels up through your legs, your trunk, your shoulders, and down your arms, remember the most peaceful place you have ever been. If you prefer, create a special dream place where there is beautiful scenery—an imaginary place where you control the events and have no cares or troubles. Be sure to involve all five senses and your whole thinking/feeling system in this scene. Let this feeling of peace and tranquility surround you and support you totally and safely as the energy rises into your neck and head.

Inhale, and imagine a golden-white light shining down from above your head. Let this soothing light energy pour into the top center of your head, your crown chakra, as if the spiritual energy in your aura were pouring in like a gentle waterfall. Let it cascade down through your body, bringing light and love into your total being.

As you exhale, allow this refreshing energy to push all the remaining tension out through your hands and feet and into the chair, or bed. Visualize the tension as darkly colored energy patterns and watch it flow out from your body, through the floor, and into the crust of the earth.

Silently ask your body to release the tension and enjoy the sensation of the refreshing "ki" energy flowing through your body and aura. Feel the golden glow of your etheric body, the gently swirling colors of your astral body. Allow yourself to experience the sensation of total relaxation within the protective bubble of your whole aura by visualizing yourself inside a 12-foot ball of radiant light, feeling peaceful and tranquil. Expand your mind's energy until it completely fills the aura, and imagine that you are a radiant ball of consciousness.

> To work with this image as a shorter, separate exercise, visualize your mind as a small ball of light energy inside your forehead; direct it into the center of your head, and expand it to about four inches in diameter. Continue expanding it until it is between 12 and 16 inches in diameter and extending beyond the limits of your skull. You will feel a warm glowing halo around your head, accompanied by a feeling of increased mental awareness. Finally, direct this ball of energy down your spine until it is centered in the heart chakra, and gradually expand it until it reaches approximately 12 feet in diameter.

To end this relaxation session, take a very deep breath and silently say, "I am calm and relaxed," while registering and appreciating this statement in your head, heart, and solar plexus. Repeat this thought/feeling twice more and use it as a mantra or prompt for returning to this state of deep relaxation another time. Practice this exercise as often as possible and reinforce it by using the prompt each time. The body can learn to redirect energy just as it learns to perform other functions, like balancing on a bicycle or operating an automobile. With practice, eventually the body will respond instantly without the prior lengthy relaxation process whenever you signal it with the phrase, "I am calm and relaxed." In time, the benefits of the relaxation exercise can be realized by taking three deep breaths while silently repeating the phrase three times before each psychic Tarot reading.

INCREASE THE FLOW AND VIBRATION OF ENERGY

Following the relaxation exercise above, begin to open the chakras and circulate the energy throughout the aura. Visualize the energy flowing into the top of your head as overflowing, and gently pouring around your head. Let it form a halo of vibrant yellow energy completely around your head. Activating this image will open and energize the crown chakra.

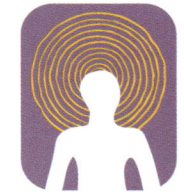

Within this crown chakra halo, mentally create a special channel—an exhaust port—for releasing unwanted energies from your aura. This special channel can handle the dense energy patterns that are freed in self-healing work. It can also help prevent the absorption and retention of energy associated with the release of a seeker's problems. An easy type of releasing visualization is to imagine a tube extending out through either side of the crown chakra. Once you have established which side is more comfortable as your exhaust port, use your exhalations as the force that sends the unwanted energy from your aura out and into space. Imagine it shooting out toward the sun where it is transformed into golden energy that falls back to earth as glittering healing energy.

After opening the crown chakra, focus your mind on each of the remaining six chakras with the intention of opening and activating each one. Imagine each chakra as a three-inch ball of energy that becomes more active and expands to five or six inches in diameter. You might visualize a set of doors opening inward from the back of the spine, or sense a color associated with each chakra glowing brightly as you focus on that part of your spine.

Experiment with different techniques until you find a personal system that is comfortable for you. You can use images, colors, sounds, sensations, or words. The main idea is to direct your mind to the chakra you desire to open; it will respond accordingly.

As you connect your mental energy to each chakra, pay close attention to the sensations you experience because you are studying your own system of body/mind signals. As you open each energy center, allow it to be healed by releasing unwanted energy up the spine and out through the exhaust port that you created in your crown chakra.

CONNECT TO A HIGHER SOURCE

Use the relaxation exercise to expand the mind's energy until it fills the crown chakra. Bring this expanded ball of light down to the solar plexus and feel in your gut the desire to be protected and guided by a higher source. Project this desire up the spine and out through the third eye chakra, as if you were sending a telepathic message on a beam of concentrated light. Then, in an attitude and position of prayer, remain as focused in the solar plexus as possible while you imagine a beam of gold light shining down to you from your higher self. Try to feel the warmth in your skin as it enters the back of your neck, down through your spinal column, and throughout your aura. When your gut feels a sensation of warmth, expansiveness, or other positive energy signal, you are connected. You may also experience other sensations associated with being connected, such as heat or vibrations in your body (e.g., hands), light-headedness, or gentle pulsations in your chakras.

It is necessary to project outside your own aura if you want to become a psychic channel. If you do not have a system of spiritual beliefs, you should focus on the highest forms of love, wisdom, and positive power possible. If you align your desire for spiritual connection with your personal religious beliefs, you will be starting from a higher path. A very practical system for psychic Tarot readings is to call on your personal spiritual guides, or guardian angels, after connecting to your higher self.

> Personal spiritual guides, or guardian angels, represent states of consciousness dedicated to assist human spiritual development and to ease human suffering on this plane.

As you gradually open to nonphysical reality you will feel a new excitement about your capabilities and tremendous joy from sharing your findings with others. It is the beginning of another leg of the journey into spiritual awareness.

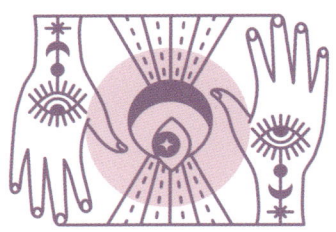

AVOIDING COMMON PROBLEMS ON THE PATH

Some common problems that occasionally develop on the path to greater psychic awareness are fear reactions, internal conflicts over semantics or techniques, self-aggrandizement, and the "sponge" syndrome. All four problems are usually caused by a lack of understanding by the student/reader. The basic solution to these, as well as to other problems that may be encountered, is to learn more about the subject being practiced and to "know thyself." It is important to keep your mind open to new information, yet maintain a sense of emotional balance and clearheadedness throughout your development. Diligent study combined with patience, honest introspection, and continuous self-healing mark the balanced student.

FEAR REACTION

A fear reaction usually results from experiencing something not previously encountered or from reaching into an area for which you are unprepared. For example, sometimes students are afraid when they first see an aura or other clairvoyant perception.

INTERNAL CONFLICTS

Internal conflicts regarding whether or not a concept or technique is correct can usually be solved by internal negotiations. If new ideas are clashing with preconceived ideas, or different opinions are confusing you, simply allow for more than one way to be possible by remembering that many roads lead to a single destination. Every proponent of a religion, philosophy, or system of psychic development will have a unique vocabulary and methodology. Each will also have a core of basic truth that runs through all systems of higher learning. Rather than argue the dissimilarities, build upon the similarities in truth that are discovered.

SELF-AGGRANDIZEMENT

The problem of self-aggrandizement is the result of failing to see psychic abilities in their proper perspective. By remembering that the occasionally sensational information that results from psychic readings is channeled, these periods of egocentricity can be minimized. Also, remember that ultimately it is the patients who heal themselves.

THE "SPONGE" SYNDROME

Many readers claim that they personally feel the seeker's troubles and pains long after the reading is over. They describe themselves as "sponges" for other people's problems and need to find a way to become less affected. This absorption of negative energy is usually the result of the reader being open to the energy of the seeker, without being open as a channeling healer. If the reader opens his or her aura to healing energy from a higher source, while maintaining an exhaust port in the crown chakra, this personal absorption will be reduced. When the reader is properly channeling healing energy from a higher source, both parties walk away from a reading feeling refreshed and rejuvenated.

TECHNIQUE FOR SELF-HEALING

After preparing for psychically-oriented work by using the techniques to relax, energize, and connect, place your hands together and gently rub your palms against each other. Visualize a stream of energy entering your crown chakra on the opposite side of your exhaust port and flowing down to your arms and to your hands. Create a sense of concentrated healing energy passing through your hands and place your hands over the front of each chakra, one by one.

You may feel warm, powerful energies passing through your hands and throughout your body and feel streams of dense energies flushing out of your aura via the exhaust port. You might also imagine green energy rising from the bottom of your aura and bathing you in waves of green healing energy from the loving energy of nature. Allow your intuition to guide you through the experience and bring you to a clearer state of mind and body.

CHAPTER THREE
PSYCHIC RECEPTION

Psychic reception is the act of obtaining and becoming aware of information in an intuitive way. The information, which accurately describes a person or situation, arrives at the conscious level of the mind spontaneously as mental impressions, images, ideas, or sensations. It is not obtained through physical observation, calculation, or logical reasoning, though this does not mean the information received is illogical or impossible to reach through observation or calculation. Rather, it is the way these ideas flash into the conscious mind, as a sort of revelatory experience, that makes them unique.

The actual process of receiving psychic flashes can be viewed as the acquisition of inspired information by a person in a state of open-mindedness. The pathway of psychic energy/information is from the higher self, through the body consciousness, to the conscious mind. The body converts the energy and relays information to the mind as ideas with which it is familiar. Rarely is a reader confronted with a concept that is totally strange or inconceivable; in most cases, information received is already translated into familiar terms or recognizable symbols. Students in the early stages of practicing psychic reception, however, may have difficulty understanding how the subconscious communicates ideas to the conscious mind. As students progress they receive the majority of psychic impressions in a clear form that they can easily identify and express.

In psychic Tarot readings, insight gained through psychic reception may be blended in with information gained from observation of the seeker's mannerisms, comments, and body language, as well as from other sensory input. However, it is important that psychic readers distinguish between inner and outer experience and learn to express psychic information without being too reliant on mental observations. Seekers sometimes play "roles," either consciously or unconsciously, and readers need to be alert to this possibility.

Psychic information can be received in a form similar to any one of the five senses. The reader may see visions, hear thoughts, feel, taste, or smell in the process of receiving information psychically. When psychic impressions are received in an undefined way, it is called sensing.

LEARNING TO HEAR CLEARLY

Your psychic self is heard as a voice inside your head. The ability to hear an internal voice is not a phenomenon but part of the process called thinking, and listening to word messages being processed inside your head is another normal, everyday experience.

CLAIRAUDIENCE

Clairaudience, the clear hearing of nonphysical reality, is part of the same system, only it is used to inform the mind of psychic information. Instead of the subconscious sending personal messages to the mind, it relays psychic knowledge. The challenge in clairaudient reception is differentiating one from the other. Psychic messages are heard differently and have a different feeling associated with them. When inspired thoughts pass through the mind, they register their higher vibrations as varying tonal qualities. As a general rule, the more spiritual the source of the information, the more beautiful and the more subtle the auditory experience.

The initial stage of clairaudient development begins with differentiating psychic information from everyday mental chatter. As receptivity improves, this intuitive information is heard in a more distinct "inner voice" imparting knowledge to the mind. The highest form of clairaudience is revealed in the accounts of great teachers and leaders who have reported hearing the voice of God, or angelic beings, as a clear, external, auditory experience.

DEVELOPING CLAIRAUDIENCE

Awareness of feelings in the solar plexus can be used as one focal point for the mind in the development of clairaudience. Energy felt in the gut area is sensed as an idea rising up the spine and then into the conscious mind as an inspired thought. Another method is to create a listening area an inch or two outside your physical ear by holding a conch shell there, for example, or simply your hand. Focusing on listening to a place outside your physical body in your aura reduces interference from the personal mind chatter experienced within your head.

Other forms of interference should be considered when working with clairaudient reception. For example, if you are having psychological problems, your thoughts reflect this. If your mind is not open to a subject, you will not want to hear about it. If you are tuned into a negative vibration, you will be picking up on those frequencies. When you give readings, remember that your spine is the antenna for receiving nonphysical energy, and your thoughts and feelings determine the frequency by attracting similar vibrations. By opening your mind and having positive attitudes, thus acting as a channel for higher vibrations, your consciousness will become aware of inspired thoughts.

Let your thoughts be inspired when you give Tarot readings. Allow the cards to interact with your psychic self, and listen to your inner voice. The Tarot cards hold a wealth of knowledge, stored in symbolic, or coded, form. When the energy in the images on the cards passes through your intuitive system, it is analogous to playing an audio file through a device. In both cases it helps if the speaker system is on, or the headphones plugged in.

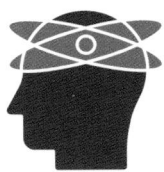

LEARNING TO SEE CLEARLY

Clairvoyance (French for *clear seeing*), in its highest stage of development, is the direct viewing of nonphysical reality. A person who has mastered clairvoyance to this degree is able to see spiritual entities in the higher planes and the human aura as easily as one sees a rock or a tree. At its simplest stage, clairvoyance is the internal viewing of images that symbolize ideas. Average clairvoyant ability falls somewhere between the two extremes.

TEST YOUR INNER VISION

The fundamental function of inner vision is to receive ideas and convert them into images. Authors rely on their written words to form images in the minds of their readers as well as to transmit ideas through direct verbal messages. Comedians tell stories that evoke humorous images in the minds of the audience.

Test your inner vision with the following: Try not to see a pink hippopotamus wearing a yellow ballet outfit (with purple polka dots), sporting a matching parasol. Furthermore, don't see her smiling at you and waving to get your attention as she dances atop a white picket fence.

Because of the colorful description and the humorous character, this vision obviously and clearly comes to mind, especially if you are trying not to see it.

DREAM WHILE AWAKE

Receiving psychic visions is a form of dreaming while awake. As an altered state of consciousness, it can be compared to having one foot in the physical world and the other in nonphysical reality, with your mind alert to visual information. Visual psychic reception is clearest when the mind is flowing along the edge of sleep, without actually falling into it. Learning to remain flowing along this boundary while remaining awake will develop your ability to maintain brainwaves in the alpha level, an altered state of consciousness that is best suited for psychic reception. Deep relaxation is beneficial to clairvoyant perception also.

When people are in the sleep stage, they are unaware of the images flashing on the mind's screen. In the morning they usually remember only a small percentage of the visual experience. Later in the day it may be completely forgotten. Similar experiences are reported by clairvoyant psychic readers. As soon as a reading is over, the images seen begin fading from their memory into a forgotten dream sequence, as if the readers had been dreaming while awake.

CREATE AN INTERNAL VIEWING SCREEN

A good way to provide a clear space for receiving psychic images is to create an internal viewing screen. "Internal," in this instance, refers to the location within the aura, but outside the physical body. Bringing the screen into the astral body helps reduce interference from personal images and thoughts experienced inside the head.

A "viewing screen" is just a tool. Before creating one, identify how you "see" now. You may "see" as if you are directly observing a scene, either in front of, or above it. If you are comfortable with your own system of seeing, there is certainly no need to change it. You might want to experiment with this method however.

Create a mental image of a screen about six to twelve inches in front of your eyes. Imagine a white rectangular surface with gold borders around it or create a television set with full controls for changing the subject being viewed, fine-tuning the picture, even adding sound to the experience if you wish. Form the screen system that is best suited to you.

Begin practicing using your screen by seeing an image of an object that is familiar to you, such as a pencil. Hold the vision and use your thoughts to maintain a clear picture of it. Try to keep it from tumbling or fading from view. The object should remain stable, clear, and be controlled by your mind's directions. In time you can even ask your psychic self to write messages to you using this pencil. Practice seeing other objects, places, or people that are also familiar.

Use this screen to gain insight into your personal needs and as a tool for clairvoyant psychic reception. It can prove to be a useful device for objectively viewing messages sent from your subconscious

> Crystal balls are sometimes used as viewing screens in clairvoyant readings. They allow psychics to visually relax into the space within the ball to perceive visions.

self regarding your personal growth. Symbols, objects, characters, and detailed scenes viewed on the screen can provide helpful information to support and enhance messages in the cards during your Tarot readings.

USING THE OTHER SENSES

Clairsentience incorporates the remaining three senses as vehicles for transmitting psychic knowledge to the conscious mind. The emotions can intermix with the senses of taste, smell, and touch and contribute to an internal experience that reveals information of a psychic nature. For example, the reader may experience sadness coupled with the physical feeling of a lover's goodbye embrace, perhaps accompanied by the taste of salty tears and the smell of a flower garden in early spring, indicating a sad parting of two people. Further details of this event could be obtained by opening the mind to intuitive ideas regarding this parting and speaking spontaneously about them.

For a full-spectrum effect the reader could employ the senses of sight and sound as well. This could be done by desiring a vision of the parting scene and either listening in on the conversation or listening to the inner voice narrating the scene. This whole mechanism demonstrates how the creative imagination can be engaged in receiving psychic information.

BECOMING AWARE OF GUT FEELINGS

The greater the number of sources of information, the greater the accuracy of the reading. As a rule, psychic readers should connect their gut feelings into each and every impression, whatever the source, to validate the information. The solar plexus will always have a response to the mind's interpretation of these psychic messages. Gut feelings are body responses localized in the solar plexus. As described in the previous chapter, the sensations in the gut can range from a vague sense of energy flow to a wrenching pain. Gut responses are sometimes thought of as an animal/human system retained from the caveman period that warns of the presence of danger. This same area of the body can be trained to respond in a highly sophisticated way as an energy sensor and converter finely tuned to nonphysical reality.

On a psychic level, body consciousness senses exactly what is needed to ensure continuous growth in all aspects of a person's life. It is attracted to the people who will prove to be helpful and is repelled by those who are harmful to the soul's path of development. This attraction/repulsion mechanism also functions to direct the mind regarding situations that are positive or negative as growth experiences. There are even gut reactions to simple physical objects such as books, cars, electronic equipment, and clothing.

A few important points should be considered when gut feelings are depended upon to direct the mind's decisions. First, the ultimate responsibility for all decisions rests with the conscious mind. Second, the best direction for learning should be chosen on the basis of it fulfilling the "incarnational plan" and providing optimal spiritual growth. Third, and most important, the degree of accuracy of the gut reactions and the clarity of mental reception is directly proportional to the extent of psychological development of the subconscious self.

> The "incarnational plan" is the potential life situations chosen by the spirit before incarnating, designed to provide fulfillment of spiritual growth. On a body/subconscious level, it is similar to a program in a computer's memory.

To develop a personal system of psychic signals, you can explore simple yes/no gut responses. First, go through the three-stage relaxation exercise described in the last chapter to open yourself for psychic work. Then close your eyes and place both hands over your solar plexus. Now, to experience your signal for "Yes," concentrate on an image that is positive for you such as hugging your child, winning the sweepstakes, completing an important task, or eating your favorite food. Feel the energy flow down from your head and into your solar plexus and notice the response your gut has to this image. Try this with different items toward which you have positive feelings and write down the various types of "Yes" reactions you experience in your gut. Try to be precise in your descriptions. To define your signals for "No," do the same exercise with images that you know are not enjoyable or beneficial to you. In time you can draw up an extensive list of your own system of gut reactions to various items, to which you can continuously add and refine by observing subtle shifts in gut energy in myriad circumstances.

Developing an increased awareness of the gut-to-head signaling system is a practical tool for psychic Tarot readers. The gut sensations the reader feels can be used as a navigational aid to help direct the course of a reading. They will draw the reader to focus on certain aspects of the cards in a spread, for example, or to zero in on one meaning instead of another, and the feelings indicate whether the information being given is on target.

OTHER WAYS TO RECEIVE PSYCHIC INFORMATION

Learning to perform different types of psychic readings opens new ways of receiving psychic information in a Tarot reading. All of the following types of psychic readings can be incorporated into a Tarot reading.

PSYCHOMETRY

Psychometry is the reception of psychic information by touching, or focusing on, a physical object. The reader concentrates on an object, tunes into the vibrations that are in it, and receives psychic impressions pertaining to the owner of the object. This type of reading can be performed on the new energy vibrations that enter the Tarot cards during the handling of the deck by the seeker, or by holding an object belonging to the seeker while the cards are being mixed and cut.

PICTURE READING

Picture reading involves concentrating on a photograph to connect to a person in the same way as in psychometry. It trains a psychic to receive impressions from a two-dimensional representation of a person. This can also be applied to Tarot cards by focusing on a court card and speaking about the character being represented by that particular card.

Both types of readings—psychometry and picture reading—can be practiced to identify a Tarot reader's personal system of psychic receptivity and to increase psychic abilities in general. A Tarot reader can also hold an object or photograph of a person in the seeker's life who is not present to provide psychic information seen in the cards relative to that individual.

AURA READING

An aura reading is the psychic interpretation of a person's energy. This type of reading is performed by focusing on the energy around a person's body and psychically converting this energy into information. The reader feels the energy, senses the colored energy patterns, and/or actually sees the colors of the aura. All three ways of perception involve bringing higher energy through the chakras and describing psychic impressions that result from being connected to the energy of the seeker's aura.

TECHNIQUE FOR SEEING AN AURA

To see an aura you must allow your eyes to relax and go out of focus while bringing in energy through the top center of the crown chakra, down to the solar plexus, and up to and out through the third eye chakra. To relax the eyes means to look at something while also visually taking in everything around it. For example, close this book and place it about six feet away from where you are sitting. Look at the cover while simultaneously noting the ceiling, both walls, and all the objects within range of your peripheral vision. The details of the cover will become fuzzy, and you may experience a slight light-headedness. In order to see an aura, use this same type of relaxed vision while looking at the air space a few inches above someone's head. You can practice this by looking at your own aura in a mirror. Look for a white/yellow glow around your head while you remain as relaxed as possible.

When two people meet, they each make subconscious evaluations by sensing the energy of the other, though they are not aware of the psychic methods employed. Gut feelings, emotional signals, and psychic impressions are the body's way of identifying and expressing the character and state of mind of another person. In a Tarot reading this information can be brought to a more conscious level and used in conjunction with the cards simply by being open to the seeker's energy throughout the session.

Practicing each type of psychic reading will enhance your psychic abilities and help you in your personal and professional growth. Even if you are not planning to give professional psychic Tarot readings, insight and healing can be gained by developing all of your psychic talents. The reader is a channel for higher information and healing energy needed by the seeker. The more open the psychic reader is, the greater the flow of both insight and energy. No matter what type of reading is being given, the reader should be sensitive to the unspoken needs of the seeker and allow intuitive impressions to flow across a bridge of warm, healing energy.

CHAPTER FOUR
THE MAJOR ARCANA AS A SPIRITUAL JOURNEY

I have woven the 22 cards of the Major Arcana into a story to facilitate learning the messages they impart. (See page 12 for a basic explanation.)

0 A young boy leaves his hometown and begins a long journey, carrying his life possessions on a stout rod. He travels aimlessly across the countryside in search of spiritual truth. He stops at the small village of Rota where he is taunted and called **THE FOOL** by the children and old men alike. They say he is a naive young man with an overly imaginative mind who speaks of unimportant things and unrealistic ideals. The boy realizes his vulnerability and need for caution. He knows a decision must be made. He searches within himself for inner guidance, and chooses to leave Rota and travel northward toward the forbidden mountains.

I As he travels onward he misses the warm fires at home and is weary from the many months on the road, but he presses on determined to translate his ideas into actions and direct his own life. Upon seeing a small school of the occult set alone in the foothills, he takes the initiative and seeks admission. He becomes an apprentice. After many years of diligent studies, he acquires the skill and confidence to develop his psychic abilities and displays the wise and honorable use of them, thus earning the title of **THE MAGICIAN.** As he prepares to leave the school, he knows he is about to begin a new and successful cycle in his life.

II Before leaving, however, he seeks out the understanding and loving **HIGH PRIESTESS.** Through her intuitive guidance and spiritual inspiration, he gains knowledge and wisdom. She shares with him the esoteric teachings that are contained in the secret scrolls she protects.

III He treks to the city where he is given audience at the royal court. The loving and devoted **EMPRESS** offers him all the comforts and luxuries of the castle during his stay in the city. In a motherly way she teaches him three axioms: creativity, practical action and productivity. She wishes him good luck, prosperity and happiness during his lifetime.

IV **THE EMPEROR**, a highly intelligent and reasonable man, counsels the young man about using mental control to govern the emotions, and presents him with the royal seal of authority to carry with him on his journey.

V **THE HIEROPHANT** in the city listens to the young man's questions with compassion and instructs him in regard to tradition and orthodoxy. During a religious ceremony, he prays for guidance and inspiration for the youth and blesses him and his spiritual venture.

VI   The young man briefly returns to his home town to speak to the girl with whom he has joined hearts in love since his childhood days. He tells her how often he thought of her beauty, her inner harmony, and her caring and trusting ways during his travels away from home. As **THE LOVERS** embrace, they discuss his future travels away from her. He explains his need to continue his spiritual journey and kisses her goodbye. He knows he has to control his emotions and make responsible decisions based upon spiritual values.

VII   The young man understands and controls the opposing forces within him during this difficult situation. His father takes him to the edge of the wilderness in his **CHARIOT**, and the young man sets out on his journey again, knowing that only his self-control and perseverance will bring success and triumph in the end.

VIII   Through inner **STRENGTH**, courage, patience and persistence, he applies his mental powers to overcome the many adverse conditions he encounters in crossing the land and the dangerous foothills to climb the mountain to the cave where a wise man lives alone.

IX   He receives good counsel from the wise man who lives as a **HERMIT** at the top of the lonely mountain. The young man is told to withdraw for a period of seven years and enter into meditations that will provide him insight and inspiration.

X In his meditations he enters into the calm center of the **WHEEL OF FORTUNE** to learn to accept the constant cycles of growth and the perpetual changes of life as a natural part of destiny and karma, and he sees future visions of growth, success and good fortune.

XI The young man knows he must pass through a time of trial and tribulation if he hopes to achieve balance and inner harmony. He sits before the karmic scales of **JUSTICE**, having accepted responsibility for his decisions and actions in life.

XII Knowing he must release his past patterns in order to continue his spiritual growth, he accepts the symbol of **THE HANGED MAN** as his new ideal of noble sacrifice and faith. He spends many months of soul-searching to prepare himself to adjust to new ideas and conditions, knowing that his reward will be inspiration and inner peace.

XIII He falls ill with a sudden fever and battles feelings of failure and loss and begins to undergo a traumatic change. He realizes that he must release all prior knowledge and welcome the **DEATH** of his old self in order to make way for a major transformation and the birth of higher consciousness.

XIV He remembers the many lessons he was taught, that a mature individual must acquire the quality of **TEMPERANCE**. He must harmonize the psychic and spiritual forces and master self-control and moderation and learn to adapt to whatever life may offer.

XV	While in the throes of fever, he sees a vision of **THE DEVIL** who tempts him with all the physical pleasures, money and power of the material world. The man exercises caution and struggles with his lusts and fears and fights the destructive forces, bad habits and evil influences holding him in bondage.
XVI	At the peak of the fever, an unforeseen catastrophe befalls him. Still caught in the internal struggle, he feels his failure, loss and the pain of his severed relationship and, in delirium, stumbles over the low balcony of the retreat in **THE TOWER** and falls.
XVII	As he lies on the ground, he looks up and sees a shining **STAR** and is miraculously filled with insight, courage, inspiration and enlightenment from his spiritual self. He sees a time of new hope and wonderful visions of the future as he receives a spiritual healing of body and mind.
XVIII	A few hours later the occult forces of the rising **MOON** play upon his imagination, making him aware of his past fears, disillusionment, emotionality, and his yearning for security and fulfillment. He feels the full import of the harsh and perilous period he passed through and sees visions of deception and problems for his loved ones back home.
XIX	The next morning the man awakens to the warmth, light, love and joy of the shining **SUN**. He reviews his achievements and his new growth, and he feels contentment and happiness throughout his entire being. It is a brand new day.

XX The man realizes his point of view has changed from the purely personal to an awareness of cosmic influences and an understanding of his role in the scheme of things. He rises to his knees and prays aloud for healing and atonement and calls out to the higher realms for his final **JUDGEMENT** and liberation.

XXI An overwhelming sense of security, peace, lasting joy and spirituality fills him as he packs his scant belongings and places them into a small sack that he flings over his shoulder. Having found that all he sought was inside his heart all the time, he sees it is time for a change, and he prepares to travel back to his small village, feeling he has finally earned recognition and prosperity. Celebrating his success and liberation, he sets out again into **THE WORLD** to share his mystical revelations.

0/XXII As he comes into the village of Rota again, he stops by the well for a drink and speaks to the villagers there. He shares what he has learned of wisdom and love of the creative mind and open heart and further of being in touch with the higher mind and the need to follow inner guidance in making decisions. He is now a mature seeker who has attained a high degree of consciousness. Many people gather around him as he describes his spiritual journey. Many feel hope in their hearts as they listen to him, but the children and old men alike continue to call him **THE FOOL**.

CHAPTER FIVE
THE MAJOR ARCANA

0. THE FOOL (ALPHA)

Description: A young man gazes into the distance as if into the future, as he walks along. Preoccupied with his thoughts and dreams, he pays no attention to the problems or potential dangers he may encounter in the immediate vicinity.

He is warmly dressed in layers of clothing and wears a jaunty orange cap with feathers hanging toward the right side. All of his worldly belongings are tied into a cloth (not shown on card) attached to the end of the walking stick he carries over his right shoulder. The walking stick, a budding rod, has the potential for fully realized blossoms. It is friend and protector to him in his travels, his spiritual strength and resource.

The single white rose in his right hand symbolizes his purity and innocence. Though he walks on the earth, his head is in the clouds. His good intentions and innocence are counteracted by his lack of caution and wisdom. He personifies the unrealized potential for the attainment of cosmic consciousness in all humans.

The designation of 0 on the card is both the shape of the cosmic egg and the symbol for eternity. It suggests both nothingness and unlimited potential.

Meaning: Portrays an open and highly imaginative mind, yet suggests vulnerability due to immaturity, naivete, and unrealistic ideals. As a card of events, can indicate an important choice and the need for caution, inner guidance, and wisdom in the decision.

Reversed: Foolishness, carelessness, weakness, excessiveness, intoxication, irrationality, even madness. Misguided thinking leads to a foolish decision.

1. THE MAGICIAN

Description: The Magician stands before a table upon which are the symbols for the four suits of the Minor Arcana. The Rod represents spiritual application of knowledge; the Sword, the use of mental powers to overcome obstacles; the Cup, the understanding of the emotional plane; and the Pentacle, the accomplishment on the material or physical plane. The presence of the four symbols on the Magician's table represents his mastery of the four planes of the earth and his ability to deal with any life situation.

The cosmic lemniscate, the symbol for infinity, is suspended horizontally over the Magician's head in the area of his crown chakra, symbolizing infinite wisdom in touch with the human mind. His belt, formed by a serpent swallowing its tail, another image for infinity, suggests the sublimation and application of eternal energy through the body. His wand to his left, actually a second Rod, illustrates the mastery of spiritual energy and the ability to use it on the earthly plane. In the upper corners of the card are triangles (the alchemical symbol for fire); circles (the symbol for the sun); and plant leaves, indicating his attunement to nature and acceptance of the cycles of life.

The Magician represents the power of reasoning and the ability to communicate ideas. He embodies effort, self-control, willpower, understanding, and the wise application of divine guidance to overcome difficulties and master any life situation. Through clear thinking and mental visualization, the Magician harnesses his creative energy and directs it with his will. He is a fully-realized human being committed to the path of higher knowledge.

Meaning: Portrays a person who is wise, skillful, confident, and has initiative and willpower. Represents the ability to translate ideas into actions, deal with difficulties, and to control and direct one's life. Also reveals the mastery of psychic abilities and their wise and honorable use. Can indicate the beginning of a new and successful project or life cycle.

Reversed: Incompetence, uncertainty, lack of willpower, deceit, manipulation. The abuse of power for selfish gain or destructive purposes. Can indicate a period of bad luck.

2. THE HIGH PRIESTESS

Description: The High Priestess gazes at a butterfly resting on the flowers she holds in her left hand. The flowers symbolize beauty and the potential for growth in all life forms. The butterfly, the symbol for intuition and

movement, is within her domain.

She wears a three-tiered headdress with an abstract cross shape as its frontpiece. Her robe is a dark material with a print of upright oak leaves, symbolic of her strength and spirituality. The scarlet veil above her head is decorated with pomegranates, symbolizing fertility, productivity and complexity.

Beside her are the scrolls of ancient wisdom, the books of occult teachings that are under her protection. These scrolls are contained within two vessels in the shape of pillars, representing the law of opposites and the ability to use the knowledge within for either good or evil; hence her role as protector and arbitrator of its release.

In the distance across a wide body of water is a castle set in a niche between the mountains, a spiritual center offering higher knowledge and tranquility. The mountains are reflected on the water just as the wisdom of the higher forces are reflected in the subconscious.

The High Priestess guards the entrance to the school of occult knowledge. She symbolizes the hidden influences that affect seekers on the path and the secret teachings that they must learn. She embodies femininity, introspection and the role of the subconscious mind as a channel for the higher teachings. She represents the development of intuition and the psychic senses as well as their correct application for the betterment of the soul.

Meaning: Embodies the feminine principles of creativity, understanding, self-reliance, serenity, and love. Represents education, knowledge, wisdom, secrecy, and esoteric teachings. Can stand for intuition, foresight, spiritual inspiration, and refer to events being affected by positive hidden influences.

Reversed: Portrays a shallow-minded and insecure woman who is insincere, selfish, and conceited. Physical passions, self-destructiveness, negative hidden influences.

3. THE EMPRESS

Description: The Empress faces forward looking intently at the viewer. She wears a crown containing twelve stars, which represent the twelve signs of the zodiac and her rulership over time. Her violet cape implies her spiritual protection.

In her right arm she cradles a wooden scepter. It is topped with a sphere, which symbolizes her rule over conditions and situations within the physical plane. In her left hand she holds a shield engraved with the astrological symbol for the planet Venus; it represents the integration of physical and spiritual love, harmonious energies, and a high sense of values. Ripened wheat grows to her right, symbolic of her relation to nature and her ability to reap the harvest of life. A waterfall flows down from the barren cliffs behind her. Water, the maternal giver and preserver of life, symbol of the great reservoir of unconscious knowledge, flows down from above, suggesting potential; and pools below in the valley where it promises fertility and productivity in the Empress's realm.

The Empress typifies the feminine ruling power that provides order, creativity and productivity to the world. She also portrays the subconscious mind and the positive force of emotions. She is guided by her intuition and uses her inner strength to rule over her domain with devotion and affection.

Meaning: A loving and devoted family woman who is the essence of creativity and productivity. She represents initiative and practical action that brings success, comfort, luxury. Good luck, prosperity, and happiness. Can also indicate fertility and motherhood.

Reversed: An unhappy and selfish woman representing poverty and disruption of the home or social setting. Indecision, wastefulness, sterility, bad luck.

4. THE EMPEROR

Description: The Emperor sits upon his throne, the seat of power and authority, before lavender flowers that are fully blossomed, except for the flower nearest his heart. The throne's uprights are made of carved rams' heads, facing in opposite directions. The ram represents the astrological sign of Aries, which governs the head, face and brain and indicates intelligence, individuality, strength and authority. The Emperor can understand opposing views and fairly decide the best course of action to be taken.

His orange crown is fitted over a studded brown cloth that drapes down the center of his body to border his chakras, suggesting his energetic mind ruling over the earth domain and over his body. The red jewels on his crown and third eye area indicate spiritual thoughts and visions influencing his decisions.

The scepter in his right hand is in the form of an ankh, the Egyptian cross that is the symbol for life. The orange circle forming the top of the ankh relates to active rulership by the mind. The globe in his left hand suggests order and dominion over the world and relates to his ability to use his creativity in the carrying out of his plans.

The Emperor personifies mental reasoning, organization, stability, and tangible accomplishments. He represents the masculine principles of realization, action and dominion; the ability of the human mind to carefully measure and determine the parameters of a complex situation and make the correct decision.

Meaning: A mature man of authority who is intelligent, experienced, confident and reasonable. Can indicate a dominant male influence in the seeker's life. He represents the ability to use mental control over emotions and the ability to successfully execute plans of action.

Reversed: An immature man with poor self-control who can be unreasonable. Can denote weakness of character, loss of confidence and ambition, failure to carry out ideas.

5. THE HIEROPHANT

Description: The Hierophant holds his right hand up in benediction, two fingers pointing heavenward, a sign of well-wishing and spiritual blessing. It is also a signal for invoking spiritual forces to flow into the physical plane; esoteric knowledge into the exoteric.

He wears a red three-tiered ecclesiastical hat, and to his left stands a triple cross—both symbols of high spiritual office. The tiers of his crown refer to his mind's aspiration for and attunement to the higher realms. The triple cross symbolizes the manifestation of divine fire through the lower planes; the upper two horizontal bars on the cross, a balancing on the higher rungs of the ladder of spirituality.

The two crossed keys below the figure's right arm are used to unlock the subconscious and conscious mind to receive inspired thoughts. They also represent the power of the moon and sun as forces that affect the human condition.

The Hierophant represents intuition; the communicator and translator of the higher voices; mediator between heaven and earth. He is also the protector of the teachings and traditions of the established order, and the perpetuator of orthodoxy. He stands for the ability to achieve spirituality and warns of the possibility of becoming trapped by the letter of the law.

Meaning: A compassionate person who is dedicated and helpful, yet may be ruled by tradition and orthodoxy. Can represent receiving instruction, guidance, inspiration, or the ability to hear the inner voice. Can also signify a religious ritual, such as a marriage ceremony or an initiation.
Reversed: A weak and confused person who is unorthodox but open-minded. Can indicate misguidance, receiving bad advice. Also relates to inability to hear inner voice, or falsity in same.

6. THE LOVERS

Description: Two lovers gaze deeply into each other's eyes as they embrace. The male is elaborately clothed and helmeted in bright plumage as is the male bird in nature. His cloak partially covers the female, as if to protect her. Spiritual rods blossom behind the male, suggesting he is flowering spiritually through relating to the female side of his psyche.

The female, on the far right of the card, is partially hidden by a screen decorated with triangular mountains and a fanciful tree bearing fruit growing from triangular caps. Her long flowing hair is held by an ornate headband decorated with triangles suspended from discs. The band itself has a zigzag pattern, a motif representing fire, which is energy that can be expressed on the physical as well as the spiritual plane. At the center of the headband, in the area of her third eye chakra, is an inverted triangle within a circle. The inverted triangle is the alchemical sign for water and relates to the emotions. The location of it here also emphasizes the feminine aspect of her intuition, or sixth sense.

In a broader sense, triangles stand for the joining together of two opposing forces by a third force—the man and the woman joined in union by the bond of love. It can also mean the union of male and female aspects in the human psyche, a prerequisite for the fully developed person.

Meaning: Beauty, inner harmony, a caring and trusting relationship, the joining of two hearts in love. It can also indicate the necessity for making a responsible decision which calls for emotional control and adherence to spiritual values in the choice.

Reversed: Frustration, inner turmoil, mistrust, and disagreements in a romance or marriage. Can denote irresponsibility and indecision. Also can mean avoidance of true intimacy, lust, unfaithfulness.

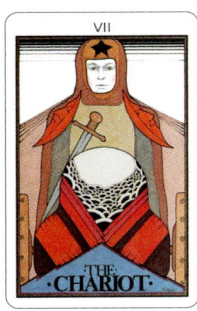

7. THE CHARIOT

Description: A strong-faced man peers out through the opening of his helmet as he drives a chariot. With determination and strength he harnesses opposing forces and guides the chariot skillfully toward his goal. On his helmet is a black, five-pointed star, a symbol of the spiritual energy he uses to oppose the forces of darkness. The color black also represents the earth and relates to primary matter; hence the sublimation of physical forces is indicated.

At his shoulders two crescent moons face away from each other; one smiling, the other frowning. They portray highly volatile contradictory forces controlled and balanced by even greater ambition and willpower. As moons they also represent the cyclic nature of change.

The unsheathed sword angled over the heart chakra of the charioteer indicates his preparedness to do battle out of the center of his being; his conscious use of mental power to fight off dark forces.

The Chariot is symbolic of the human body; the charioteer personifies the soul directing the body as well as the human mind harnessing the forces of the physical world. The studded wheels bordering the angular design of the chariot represent power and mobility.

Rows of curved symbols create a clear path through the belly of the charioteer, suggestive of an opening to the internal (subconscious) laboratory, where alchemical transmutations take place as opposing forces are kept in balance.

Meaning: A difficult situation can be controlled and directed by understanding opposing forces and bringing about balance and harmony. Self-control, personal effort, and perseverance bring an end to difficulties. Ambition, accomplishment, success, triumph.

Reversed: Lack of self-control, imbalance, poor direction, inability to handle difficulties. The use of excessive force brings defeat and dishonor. Failure.

8. STRENGTH

Description: Strength is personified by a man dressed in a highly decorative battle uniform with an unsheathed sword to his right (the side of consciousness) and a highly bred, elegant dog to his left (the side of the subconscious). The warrior looks directly ahead with an expression of courage and patience, suggesting the latent force of strength and integrity within his personality.

The unsheathed sword indicates his readiness to apply his mental powers to overcome obstacles or to defend higher consciousness. He is a man of action and purpose; prepared and calm, not impulsive and chaotic. With his strength and intelligence, he has made his dog (a symbol showing the breeding and domestication of the wild form of wolf) his ally, his loyal guardian. The warrior acknowledges messages from his subconscious that alert him to danger and help direct him.

The stones in front of the sword, stacked in three levels to form steps, suggest communication between the three levels of body, mind, and spirit; and the ascending orange tiers on the helmet echo that theme on a higher level of consciousness. True strength is strength of mind and spirit supported by the body.

Meaning: Represents inner strength, energy, courage, patience, integrity, compassion, generosity. Balance of body, mind, and spirit. The correct and persistent application of inner strength and mental powers can overcome adverse conditions in surrounding cards and bring success and honor.

Reversed: Weakness, lack of courage and integrity, corruption. Hostility, domination, abusiveness. Failure and possible loss of reputation.

9. THE HERMIT

Description: An elderly man with a long grey beard stands before a window, holding a lantern in his right hand. His face is partially hidden by a pale red hood, expressing the sublimation of sensuality and emotionality and suggesting secrecy and invisibility. Symbolically, the hood is a conical crown that envelops the entire head; therefore it stands for a mind filled with higher thoughts.

The Hermit wears a violet cloak, a loose garment that hides the definitions of his body, further emphasizing his retreat from worldly society for more spiritual pursuits. The wrists and neckline of his robes are decorated with strips of cloth in the shape of inverted elongated triangles which, at a quick glance, create the illusion of mountaintops.

The Hermit represents experience, esoteric knowledge and wisdom. He is the sage, the wise old man who has transcended his personal limitations and is willing to share his knowledge and insight to those who come to him for counsel.

The Hermit stands before a window holding a lighted lantern. The star-like radiation of the beacon shines out against the encroaching darkness of the night, lighting the way for travelers who are earnestly seeking the path of higher knowledge.

The Hermit represents the ability to become awakened and inspired when one withdraws from the influence of the outer world and seeks inspired thoughts and visions in meditation.

Meaning: A period of withdrawal and caution to reevaluate and gather inner strength. Meditation; deep reflection that provides insight, wisdom and inspiration. The need for understanding and advice. Can indicate meeting a wise person who offers good counsel.

Reversed: Withdrawal based upon fear, irresponsibility, immaturity. Can denote following bad advice, rejecting sound advice, acting hastily.

10. THE WHEEL OF FORTUNE

Description: The head of a sphinx–like figure is set upon the top of a wheel, and the winged figures of a lion and a bull face each other as they guard the wheel's base. Hebrew letters for the divine name are interspersed with arabic letters to form part of the word *taro* around the rim; alchemical symbols are written on three of the eight spokes.

Two serpents frame the opposite sides of the wheel; they represent the forces of good and evil, ascent and descent, success and failure. Here snakes also symbolize energy; their undulating patterns demonstrate the extremely high vibration associated with the working out of karmic justice through right thoughts and actions.

The Wheel symbolizes the cyclic nature of things. As the ancient symbol of the zodiac, it describes the transitory nature of movement through time. Its hub relates to the spiritual forces at the center of life and its rim to the limiting nature of the physical world; the space between the center and the circumference, the creative and the formative forces flowing from the center outward; and the spokes of the wheel, the support and communication that exists between the inner and outer worlds.

The Wheel is a mandala, a type of circular design that draws the mind towards its center as a focus for concentration and meditation. It reminds the meditator that to escape from the negative cycles experienced by those who focus primarily upon their material existence, one needs to move toward the calm center of spiritual reality.

Meaning: The end of a time of problems and the beginning of a positive cycle in one's affairs. A period of good luck, growth, expansion, success, fortune. Wishes coming true. The cycles of growth, perpetual change, destiny, karma; and the need for finding one's center of calmness.
Reversed: A time of great change that is the result of one's prior actions. Can indicate a bad turn of events,

misfortune, failure. Also indicates an unwillingness to use free will to correct problems in one's life.

11. JUSTICE

Description: Justice is a crowned woman wearing the robes of court and holding a scale in one hand and the hilt of a sword in the other. Her throne is set between two pillars created from bundles of blossomed rods representing the application of spiritual laws in administering justice.

Her crown symbolizes her authority to act in judgement regarding the obeyance of those laws. The ruby-colored jewel decorating the front of the crown signifies that she acts with enlightenment; its square shape symbolizes her control over the four elements and her sovereignty over the earthly plane.

The balance scale in her left hand (gloved in black) symbolizes the law of karma relating to good and evil, and the true nature of cause and effect. Justice is the fair and impartial weighing of truth; the pan balance tips according to the weight of evidence placed on it. The central pivot, a phallic shape decorated with a red disc, relates to the transmission of powerful cosmic forces directed for the perpetuation of life. The balanced position of the scales in this illustration points to the achievement of balance and harmony.

The sword in Justice's right hand (gloved in grey) stands for correct thinking, determination of the spirit, decisiveness, and the protection of righteousness. Sheathed in its scabbard, the sword refers also to the protection of the innocent and the use of force only when necessary.

Meaning: The achievement of balance and inner harmony after a time of trial and tribulation. An honest person with good intentions who is responsible for his or her own decisions and actions. The fair and judicious outcome of a matter or legal problem. Cosmic justice, karma.
Reversed: Lack of balance and integrity, intolerance, harshness. Making wrong decisions, and the resulting failures that ensue. Can mean injustice or an unfavorable decision in a legal matter.

12. THE HANGED MAN

Description: A stoic-faced man hangs upside down from a cross by a rope tied to his right foot. A jagged power design issues from an orange cup-like shape covering his throat. It appears to point toward his base chakra, but actually, because of the Hanged Man's inverted position, is aimed up to the heavens. The power bolt dramatizes the transformation of sexual energy into higher energy, as in the raising of the kundalini. The issuance of the arrow out of his throat chakra suggests the Hanged Man's communication of this sublimation as a conscious request rather than an action forced upon him by his unfortunate situation.

The cross, composed of living wood, is an occult symbol for cosmic life. Its upright beam symbolizes spiritual forces flowing down to the earth, and the crossbeam its balanced distribution on the earth plane. The junction of the two beams, where the foot is secured, is the power-point of this symbol. The cross also symbolizes crucifixion in the sense of the awakening that results when the mind surrenders to a higher power.

The inversion of the figure points to his reversal of prior thought and behavior patterns for the purpose of purification. He has realized the folly of following along the path of selfishness and materiality and is not afraid to be different. By releasing his past patterns to obtain an alternate view of life, he has gone through a transition and achieved spiritual awareness. The Hanged Man illustrates the rejection of the personal self for the attainment of the mystical state of mind. It relates to the mind's union with God, and the inner peace, inspiration and faith that results from alignment with the divine will.

Meaning: A major change, transition, readjustment to new ideas and conditions—ultimately for the good. Psychic awareness, intuition and spiritual wisdom as the outcome of releasing past patterns and continuing one's growth. Inner peace, inspiration, faith and noble sacrifices.
Reversed: Self-centeredness, materialistic, untrusting, lacking faith. Following conventional thought instead of one's intuition. Also false security and futile sacrifices.

13. DEATH

Description: Death is a skeleton dressed in a soldier's uniform. Although a skeleton suggests mortality, it is also the sturdy frame upon which the earth body is built, and its skull is the receptacle for thought. The skeleton is also that part of the body that remains after death, on a higher level suggesting the soul's survival after a journey through life in a physical form.

Death carries a dark brown banner upon which blooms a brown wild rose, with a rosebud pointing toward Death's destination. The brown colors of the banner and flowers emphasize man's origin from and return to the earth; the fertility of earth as well as one's mortality. The flowers symbolize the cycles of earth life. The fully blossomed flower is closer to the end of its cycle than the bud, which is at the beginning of its cycle, yet both are only minor cycles that perpetuate the growth of the total organism, the rosebush.

Death's drably colored helmet is topped with a thin red plume; a blood-red cloth, like blood itself, flows out from under the helmet down past the shoulders. Red is not only the color and symbol of blood, it also refers to the alchemical fire that transforms base forms (prime matter being black) into the superior form of pure gold, thus describing the major change in consciousness that is associated with this card; the death of the old order to make way for the new. Only through releasing past patterns of thinking, personality traits and lifestyles can a new way be opened for a better way to think and live.

Death rides past a hill as if from a battle victory. The sun rises between two towers set on the hill, symbolizing the dawning of a new day after the darkness and fear of the night.

Meaning: A major transformation. Unexpected and traumatic change in one's life, which paves the way for a positive cycle. Death and rebirth; generally applied to one's own consciousness or past lifestyle. Can represent feelings of bad luck, failure, loss.

Reversed: Stagnation, holding onto the past, and fearfully resisting change. Loss, personal failure, disorder, catastrophe.

14. TEMPERANCE

Description: Temperance is personified by an ornately winged angel who stands against a red and black background. Owl-like feathers cover her body; brown feathers hug the sides of her body, like small supplementary wings. Powerful flying wings rise from her shoulders, their long white feathers hanging parallel to the angel, forming pillars on each side of the figure. Wings relate to freedom of flight. They denote spiritual thoughts, their ability to rise toward heaven; and feathers are symbols of contemplation, belief and hope.

Temperance's black helmet has a black frontpiece that is larger than the one on the man symbolizing Strength. It relates to the higher qualities of strength that include controlling oneself through willpower. It is decorated with four sun discs, which suggests her affinity with the nurturing energies of the sun. The cup with red spokes covering her left ear symbolizes her ability to hear higher voices, her skill in clairaudience.

Temperance is the use of patience and moderation in thought, feeling and action. It is the credo of the eternal alchemist who is dedicated to the purification of the lower self and its resulting transformation into the greater self. The psychic and spiritual energies that result are harnessed and directed by intelligence, resoluteness, tact and pure intent.

Meaning: Use of self-control, moderation, patience and tact in dealing with all situations. Balancing and harmonizing the psychic and spiritual forces and applying them to physical life. Maturity, individuality, adaptability.
Reversed: Lack of self-control, impatience, confusion, imbalance. Conflicts in personal, business and spiritual affairs create scattered energies.

15. THE DEVIL

Description: The Devil squats beneath the pale light of the full moon with its bat-like wings upraised. Beneath his malevolent gaze, two human figures face away from each other, enveloped in an ocean of hellish flames. The figures are naked, stripped of form, separated from each other;

they have become faceless humanoids with animal tails, suggesting their loss of identity and their spiritual regression to a prehuman state.

The Devil appears as a he-goat whose pointed horns seem to have broken through the skin on the skull. The horns symbolize the misused power and strength of the black magician. Centered halfway between the Devil's black-tipped horns and hot red eyes is an inverted pentagram. The five-pointed star symbolizes man; inverted, it stands for wrong thinking and behavior and the blatant disregard of spiritual laws and operations. The inverted torch to the Devil's left is the burning firebrand of unrest, strife, destruction and chaos, rather than a torch to light the way of spiritual growth as it would be in the upright position.

The Devil symbolizes adversity, violence and the dark veil that obscures the vision of those who focus on the material plane to the exclusion of higher knowledge. On the other hand, according to the occultist's view, the Devil, who represents those negative powers in the psyche, the shadow in each of us, is called the guardian of the threshold, the keeper of the gate to higher knowledge. It is the personification of all the hidden passions and fears that the earnest seeker must courageously face within before passing through advanced levels of psychic and spiritual development.

Meaning: Excessive emphasis on material world and physical pleasures; lust for money and power. Living in fear, domination, bondage. Caution is indicated in personal and business affairs. Destructive forces, violence, evil influences.

Reversed: Although weakness, fear and indecision may be evident, seeking higher forces leads to realization and release from bondage. Can indicate progress in dealing with negative forces.

16. THE TOWER

Description: A storm sends crashing waves and bolts of lightning onto a tower while flames leap out of the top and upper windows of the structure. A full moon glows against a dark and swirling sky; seagulls fly away from the storm.

The Tower is analogous to a human being, its upper windows the human mind out of which it perceives the world; the crown its capacity to spiritually communicate at the highest levels. The Tower also represents man's continuous attempt to build physical structures to protect himself against the elements and his fellow man and to rise above others using material ideals. The burning tower portrays failure and destruction, demonstrating the folly of this concept; symbolic, in this respect, of the Tower of Babel. The card acts as a warning against false security and false pride and teaches that to create a link between heaven and earth, one must do so by refining that which is within, not by rising above one's fellow man through material concepts or structures.

The self is in crisis in this card. Waves crash against the foundation of the tower, symbolizing the disruption of emotions within the body. Storm clouds swirl around, portraying the turbulence on the mental plane, and the slash of white in the dark sky indicates a lack of integration between emotional aspects of the self and the spiritual and mental.

The lightning, in a narrow sense, is a destructive form of celestial fire, having ignited the fires burning within the tower (or precipitated a crisis). But it also represents the dynamic action of the higher forces upon the earth, which can wake up oneself to the need for change. Or, it can be the flash of inspiration that comes to one who, having exhausted the pathways of the personal mind, is given the gift of creative insight.

Meaning: A sudden and unforeseen disruption, catastrophe. An abrupt change in one's life—usually regarded as leading to enlightenment and a new lifestyle. Can indicate a severed relationship, divorce, failure in business or career, extensive financial losses.

Reversed: Same as above except less severe; often unnecessary and caused by oneself. Can denote lack of insight, avoiding change, thus perpetuating an oppressive condition.

17. THE STAR

Description: A peacock, a symbol of beauty and immortality of the spirit, rests on a bush that has berries in full ripeness. Overhead and centered between two barren cliffs, a multicolored and geometrically intricate star shines. Its radiance offers hope and inspiration to all who look upon it.

The Star is the symbol for a spirit shining through the problems that envelop it. The star shines brightly in a field of darkness, just as our soul is able to overcome earthly limitations and express its true spiritual nature.

Stars represent the beauty and divine wisdom of the creator of the universe and are looked upon as a source of hope and inspiration. They inspire a sense of order and a knowledge of the existence of a higher intelligence. They remind us of our short time on earth and draw forth the feeling that there must be more beyond our present comprehension, giving hope to those who glimpse the higher spiritual message contained in them.

The stars convey the message of continuity and the divine purpose of existence. A grandmother gazing at the night sky knows that her great grandchildren will stand in her place and see the same complex patterns and feel the same feelings, as did her great grandmother.

For millennia seamen have relied on the fixity of the celestial patterns to guide their ships toward distant shores. The shining star guided the three wise men to

Bethlehem in the accounts of the birth of Jesus.

The Star's message is to aspire toward the state of mind whereby you realize the cosmic light that dwells within and see its connectedness with the greater light. In a flash of inspiration you experience oneness with the cosmic light. In mysticism this is called cosmic consciousness; in Buddhism, *Satori*.

Meaning: Insight, inspiration, courage and enlightenment from the spiritual self. A time of new hopes, wonderful visions of the future, broadening horizons, realization can be from astrological influences. Healing of body and mind, health and happiness.

Reversed: Unhappiness, lost hopes, limited vision, doubt, pessimism, failure. Can indicate problems with mental outlook or physical health.

18. THE MOON

Description: The Moon, illustrated as the profile of a human face, is shown in its first quarter, waxing toward its fullness and increased influence. It rests on a greenish globe, representing the Earth, which seems to be floating in a sea of triangular crystals. A pathway is created between two rows of futuristic pillars at the bottom of the card.

The moon affects the human condition by its gravitational force due to its close proximity to the Earth.

The crust of the Earth rises to the passing of the moon overhead; the powerful ocean tides are influenced by its gravitational pull. The human body, composed mainly of water, is subject to the moon's cyclic influence. Sometimes repressed emotions rise to the surface as the moon waxes and are acted out under the influence of the full moon, including an increase of violence.

The moon is the natural satellite of the Earth and reflects the light of the sun during the night. It casts dim light on the dark landscape that promotes illusionary viewing and is connected to the imagination in this respect. The moon is sometimes considered cold-hearted and unyielding in its reflective power to make us face our inner fears and the hostility of the night environment.

The Moon is symbolic of the subconscious mind, the soul in an out-of-body experience, and the intensity of the dream state of mind. It is the feminine principle of reflection and emotionality that rules and illuminates the darkness of the night.

Meaning: Disillusionment and fear create a deep yearning for security and fulfillment. A harsh and perilous period, threatening situations, deception, possible problems for loved ones. Can relate to occult forces, increased sensitivity and imagination, intense dreams.

Reversed: Clarity, control and peace after a difficult period. Heightened psychic abilities. Overcoming temptations, trivial problems and minor setbacks.

19. THE SUN

Description: A smiling sun sends energy beams to the four corners of the earth, interspersed with bands on a white background. The full view portrayal of the sun as a smiling face expresses the loving and guiding nature of the cosmic forces.

The Sun's white face and "neck" area form the shape of a keyhole for unlocking the joyous love that is within this symbol. The two bottom rays stand for these energies touching and influencing us on a conscious (right) and a subconscious (left) level. The two top rays, and the spaces between the rays, illustrate different areas in the crown chakra.

The sun has represented the nurturing and maintenance of the Earth throughout history. It has provided an unlimited supply of light, warmth and cosmic energy to the earth. It has been the focus of worship in many cultures as a source of earthly and cosmic illumination. It dispels the chill and the dark forms of the night and lights the path ahead. Its absorption and reflection by the flowers and trees creates a colorful display of artistic beauty. It illuminates and inspires the mind and soul in its quest for growth and spirituality.

The Sun card also visually represents the process of transmutation in alchemy. Prime matter, which is black, is transformed by the glowing red embers, hot orange flames and yellow radiance of the alchemical fire into the white light of purity and illumination.

Meaning: Warmth, light, love and joy in personal and/or business life. A time of contentment, freedom from restraints, growth, achievements, success. Happiness and sincerity in a relationship or marriage; intimacy, devotion.
Reversed: Unhappiness, loneliness, depression possibly from loss of relationship. Uncertainty, failure, loss in business situation. Note: The reversed meaning can range from a weaker version of the upright, to a false sense of happiness, to unhappiness, depending on surrounding cards and interpretation.

20. JUDGEMENT

Description: The orange sun rises above large white clouds as an angel blows the trumpet to herald a new day. The banner, bearing the insignia of a cross, hangs from the front of the upraised trumpet—a sign of elevation and exhaltation of the spirit. The cross symbolizes the heavenly forces entering the earthly domain to create balance and harmony. The bottom of this cross appears to be merged into the shadowed area of the hillside, as if it were marking a graveyard.

The sky indicates the dawning of a new existence and new perspective on life. The orange sun expresses its activity as a symbol of new beginnings and new visions; it has broken through the clouds of obscurity to brighten the field of the material plane and heighten the vibration of its inhabitants.

Archangel Gabriel, the divine herald, is the angel of visions, hopes and dreams. In the Bible he appeared to the prophet Daniel (Daniel 8:16; 9:21) and to Mary (Luke 1:19, 26) in the Annunciation. He represents the divine word and is the trumpeter of the Last Judgement (Thessalonians 4:16) that raises souls into the heavenly kingdom.

Flowers and reeds form a bouquet at the trumpeter's feet. Floral bouquets are fragrant and beautiful and are offered as a sign of love and caring. Flowers are also the symbol of spring, celebrated by certain cultures and occult schools as the time of the new year. Spring heralds the awakening of the flora and fauna of the land and the beginning of another solar cycle.

Meaning: A change from a purely personal point of view to awareness of cosmic influences and one's role in the scheme of things awakening into cosmic consciousness. A time of atonement, redemption, liberation, healing fulfillment. Rising above negativity in a situation and resolving the problems associated with it.

Reversed: Disillusionment, isolation, loss in personal point of view, worry and fear, inability to resolve problems. Delays, failures and possible loss of worldly goods.

21. THE WORLD

Description: Inside a wreath is the figure of a woman wearing a turban and a full-length tunic. She stands in a white archway contained within this circle holding a flower/wand in her right hand.

The woman portrays the serenity, the devotion and the

spiritual attainment of the adept. Her head is covered by a turban, a multilayered cloth wrapping that extends well above the crown chakra. Red jewels decorate her forehead and throat, indicating the openness of her third eye and throat chakras. Her dress is an earthy olive color that has a black design tapering from the neckline to her base chakra. Lines are woven across her solar plexus and below her base chakra.

Outside the circle, occupying the four corners of the card, are the figures of the lion, bull, angel and eagle of the Bible (Ezekiel 1:10; Revelation 4:7). Astrologically they represent the four fixed signs of Leo (fire), Taurus (earth), Aquarius (air) and Scorpio (water), respectively. Leo relates to strength, courage, willpower and the "I AM" presence in the heart center. Taurus represents patience, determination, stability and the procreative forces of nature. Aquarius relates to intelligence, intuition, independence and consecration of the lower kingdoms. The eagle embodies the highest aspects of Scorpio, such as intensity, resourcefulness, fruitfulness and attaining great heights in spiritual pursuits.

Meaning: Achievement, reward, attainment of prosperity and well-earned recognition. A time of security, peace and lasting joy. Attunement of the four aura bodies to one's spirituality. Change, travel, relocation, new home—all celebrating completion, success and liberation.

Reversed: Insecurity, fear of change, stagnation, failure to achieve goals, disappointment, regret. Entanglement and confusion in one's life caused by excess focus on physical plane.

0/22. THE FOOL (OMEGA)

Description: A young man walks beneath the white light of the higher forces while looking ahead at a distant goal. He seems to be in a state of internal vision, trusting and following his own inner guidance.

He wears an orange plumed beret that extends above and beyond the circumference of his head, indicating the expansion of his mind; the warm color implies the intense activity in the area of his crown chakra.

An ornate piece of jewelry, consisting of a rectangular toppiece, three triangles and a single disc, is pinned to the beret. The triangles represent the triune forces of love, wisdom and power, and the aspiration toward unity with the cosmic. The disc, a circle, is the astrological symbol for the sun. The central channel in the disc appears to open into the Fool's left ear, suggesting his capacity for nonphysical hearing, or clairaudience.

The budding rod he carries over his right shoulder stands for his connectedness to nature and his blossoming spirituality; the white rose in his right hand symbolizes his purity of soul attained through letting go of those things in his life that kept him in bondage to his lesser self.

The number 22 designates the completed cycle and the practical application of wisdom attained. In numerology, 22 is considered one of the master numbers (11, 22, 33, 44), not usually reduced in numerological computations (e.g., otherwise 22=2+2=4).

Meaning: Portrays the creative mind and open heart of the mature seeker who has attained a high degree of consciousness. A time of being in touch with the prompting of the higher mind; following inner guidance in making decisions. Can indicate reaching the next level of cosmic consciousness or cosmic forces taking a hand in the seeker's life situations. An important aspect is the application of higher consciousness to life.

Reversed: One who has attained a higher level of consciousness, yet has become unbalanced, in some instances to the point of losing touch with physical reality. Also misuse of higher learnings and making decisions that are defensive in nature and possibly harmful to self and others.

CHAPTER SIX
THE MINOR ARCANA
THE RODS

ACE OF RODS

Description: A single rod with a sturdy shaft blooms in a field of curved symbols, which suggest receding mountain ranges as if viewed from close to the summit. The spiritual life in the rod is strong; already the right branch is flowering and a small bud on the left is beginning to blossom.

Meaning: A time of beginnings; start of a business venture, enterprise, or family situation; marriage, birth. Can indicate a journey, adventure, inheritance. Blossoming of creativity, energy, inventiveness, spiritual strength, understanding.
Reversed: False start, cancelled plans, delays, failure, deterioration. Shallow existence, depression.

TWO OF RODS

Description: A young man looks into the distance, as if into his future, while holding a pink globe in his right hand and a flowering rod in his left, which symbolizes the duality between physical life in the world and spiritual life. The pink rose crossing the lily on the shoulder patch echoes that duality. The second rod, spiritual help, is within his reach.

Meaning: Maturity, success, power and wealth, counteracted by sadness, a sense of failure, possibly mental and physical suffering. A decisive and courageous action is needed. Clairvoyance.

Reversed: Enchantment, wonder, surprise. Loss of interest, clarity, or faith in venture. Possible trouble, fear, dread of future.

THREE OF RODS

Description: A man stands alone looking into the distance, as if watching for someone's approach. He stands amidst three flowering rods that seem to grow out of a base of dark, curved symbols. He wears a ruby-studded skullcap and a flowing robe with arched symbols on its back, which suggest church windows.

Meaning: Stands for spiritual strength, practical knowledge, effort, ingenuity and enterprise. Can signify collaboration in business, partnerships, or negotiations; practical help will come. Foresight used in an undertaking; realization of hopes.

Reversed: End of hardships; troubles and disappointments cease. Can also mean help offered is unreliable; unsound advice given.

FOUR OF RODS

Description: A castle-home is set on the peak of a hill between two mountain ridges. The gateway to the home is constructed of four blossoming rods with a garland of flower blossoms draped between the outer two. The castle's moat is crossed by a stationary bridge, indicating a time of peace and security.

Meaning: Material, emotional and spiritual blessings are the reward for diligent effort and fine work; success. A time of peace and prosperity; the restful enjoyment of a harmonious life at home after a job well done.

Reversed: Meaning can remain the same, but to a lesser degree, or delayed. Also can suggest turbulence at home and the need to protect and maintain security.

FIVE OF RODS

Description: Four young men, each carrying a rod, portray confusion by looking in different directions. They are not facing the single upright rod. Three of the men have covered heads and high necklines; the fourth, standing above the others, displays an uncovered crown, an open throat and a headband with a symbol over the third eye chakra.

Meaning: Stress, confusion, turmoil. Competition, struggle for recognition and financial rewards in occupation, business venture, or personal project. At times suggests it may lead to improvement in business affairs.

Reversed: Disputes, complications, legal or contractual problems. May also indicate an ending of turmoil or strife.

SIX OF RODS

Description: A woman proudly rides a finely clad horse past a line of rods along the road. The rods are at various angles, as if being waved in a victory parade. The rider holds a single rod in her right hand, which is crowned with a laurel wreath, symbolizing success and attainment.

Meaning: Resolution of an important matter brings satisfaction and sense of honor. Completion, success, well-earned victory after many hardships. Spiritual attunement brings realization of hopes and desires. Can also signify receiving good news.

Reversed: Indefinite delay, disappointment, frustration, false hopes, false victory, false pride. Vulnerability, fear of failure, betrayal.

SEVEN OF RODS

Description: A lone man stands upon high ground defensively holding a twin-budded rod across his chest. He wears a dark cloak, gloves and a cloth cap that bulges

to the right side of his head. The six rods below the figure appear to be encroaching on his territory or to be under his protection.

Meaning: Opposition and strife in trade, business, or a matter of principle, but inner strength, courage and determination overcome all adversity and bring victory. Standing firm and guarding spiritual principles.

Reversed: Doubt, fear, anxiety and confusion. Feeling overburdened, vulnerable; the desire to retreat. Need for decisiveness and courage.

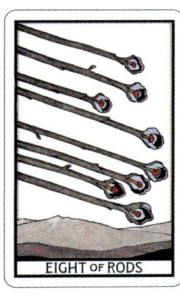

EIGHT OF RODS

Description: Eight blossoming rods traverse the open sky and descend toward the ground. The white sky forms a clear backdrop for the unhampered flight of the spiritual staves. The bottom portions of the rods are not visible, suggesting the path of flight is set.

Meaning: Progress, rapid movement toward a desired goal, and the hope for quick attainment. Can represent falling in love, or indicate traveling for business or vacation. Also signifies the spiritual journey and a sudden advancement along the path.

Reversed: Sluggish movement, delays, cancellations. Jealousy, domestic quarreling. Impatience from delays in spiritual growth.

NINE OF RODS

Description: A full-faced young man is profiled staring straight ahead as he stands guard over eight vertical rods, while holding the ninth. His spiritual strength, symbolized by the rods, will sustain and help him overcome any opposition. He wears warm, layered clothing and a white hat set with small brown stones.

Meaning: A person who is dedicated, alert and prepared to defend against adversaries. The inner qualities of strength and fortitude result from facing and overcoming opposition. Difficulties and delays may occur, but victory is indicated. Spiritual faith.
Reversed: Opposition, hardships, distress, misfortune, illness. Confusion, lack of preparedness, inability to defend oneself.

TEN OF RODS

Description: A strong man carries a heavy burden consisting of ten rods. He leans into his work as if to put his all into the task and persevere. He wears a dark brown vest over a beige shirt and a studded helmet with a white cloth hanging to his shoulder.

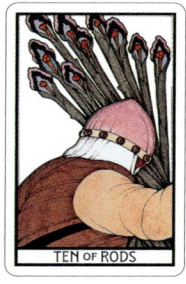

Meaning: Burdensome tasks are encountered; a person under tremendous pressure; oppressive situations; feelings of dissatisfaction, guile and remorse. Success and achievement of goals through perseverance against obstacles can be indicated.
Reversed: Difficulties encountered, opposing forces, treachery, loss. Apathy, carelessness, confusion, misdirection, self-defeat.

PAGE OF RODS

Description: A Page, looking down, walks away from a field of cattails, his posture suggesting a looking inward or a careful observation of the path he is on. He wears a wide-brimmed hat with a lavender feather pointing upward and a beige shawl draped over his shoulder.

Meaning: An honest and sincere young person who is spiritually minded. Can also stand for a growing child exhibiting family intelligence. Represents a loyal friend or lover. Portrays the bearer of good tidings, happy news, communication.
Reversed: Concern over child. Insincerity, inability to make a decision resulting in instability. Can suggest bad news or gossip.

KNIGHT OF RODS

Description: A young Knight rides holding a flowering rod over his left shoulder. A thick plume, like a stormy cloud, rises from his helmet, suggesting the turbulence he leaves in his wake. His visor is raised, indicating non-combat. His glove is decorated with arrow motifs pointing in the direction of his journey.

Meaning: A good-looking young man who is friendly and energetic, earnestly following his intuition toward spiritual goals. At times can indicate a restlessness that creates turbulence in his wake. May suggest moving on, traveling, or changing residence.

Reversed: A young man who is selfish and lacks willpower. Can indicate incompatibility, frustration, disharmony, conflict, broken relationships.

QUEEN OF RODS

Description: The Queen faces forward wearing a simple pink robe. Her hair is set in a single long braid which hangs over her right shoulder. A flowering rod stands to her right and a partly seeded sunflower to her left, indicating her spirituality and her deep connection to nature.

Meaning: A gentle, loving woman, kind and caring to all, and devoted to her family. She stands for honor, loyalty, dignity, patience, spirituality and the love of nature. May also indicate success in business or finances.
Reversed: A selfish, untrustworthy woman who is strict and controlling in money matters. Can indicate opposition, jealousy, deceit, unfaithfulness.

KING OF RODS

Description: A noble King rests his staff before him, a flowering rod with two large buds showing signs of opening, representing the continuing spiritual resources available to him. He wears a winged helmet with a silver disc on the frontpiece at the third eye chakra. The stylized bird on the helmet could symbolize Mercury, messenger of the gods.

Meaning: An honest and sincere man, kind and fair in his treatment of others. A mature man of great nobility and wisdom. He represents the qualities of loyalty, fairness and spiritual strength. Can suggest country living.
Reversed: A critical, strict and stern personality, yet sincere, tolerant and good advisor. Can indicate opposition and conflict.

THE SWORDS

ACE OF SWORDS

Description A double-edged sword is planted in the earth. A white rose blossoms on each side of the blade. The sword with its ornate hilt ringed with dark jewels is seen against a fuschia-toned, cloud-filled sky.

Meaning: The rising of powerful forces and the valiant struggle to prevail and emerge triumphant. Strength, action, great force and determination that assures success, yet may be accompanied by excessiveness and abuse. Conquest that is motivated either by love or by animosity.
Reversed: Excessive use of force resulting in weakness, confusion, chaos, self-destruction. Extremes in desires and ambitions.

TWO OF SWORDS

Description: A blindfolded young woman stands naked with two swords crossing her bosom, indicating a choice she has to make. Her way is barred by large monoliths, over which her long hair is flowing. She poses passively under clouds that have a hint of sunlight shining through them.

Meaning: Moment of decision; calm before the storm. Inability to take action, lack of clarity, indecisiveness. Can represent conforming to the dictates of authority and/or blindly following established course.

Reversed: End of period of stalemate. Caution against making wrong decision. Falsehood, disloyalty, deceit, scheming.

THREE OF SWORDS

Description: A heart is suspended in the air above a field of large monolithic structures. The heart is pierced through the front by three swords. Dark storm clouds brewing overhead are converging on the heart.

Meaning: Disappointment, distress, sorrow, emotional upheaval. Quarrels, discord, separation, absence. Division within a relationship and the mental anguish associated with the loss. Can represent choosing mental control and power over emotions.

Reversed: Turmoil, confusion, mental withdrawal and detachment, depression. Can indicate the pain of remembering past sorrows.

FOUR OF SWORDS

Description: A knight completely enclosed in a suit of armor is lying on a light blue slab with his hands interlocked. Arched church windows containing triple spheres are open to the sky. Three swords are suspended over the

knight, while the fourth is mounted on the side of the slab.

Meaning: Solitude, repose, reevaluation, recuperation. Temporary retreat from a stressful situation to gather inner strength, reorganize thoughts and make new plans. Can also portray withdrawing from the outside world to seek spiritual guidance.

Reversed: Disharmony, restlessness, procrastination. Remaining transfixed in stressful situation. Need for wise decision and cautious action.

FIVE OF SWORDS

Description: A helmeted man collects swords left after a battle. He holds one sword with his right hand; two swords rest on his left shoulder. Another two swords lie crossed on a large rock in the foreground, symbolizing that a choice is involved, or a wrong choice was made. In the distance two figures are walking away.

Meaning: Loss, defeat, destruction, dishonor. Selfishness and excessive force gives temporary victory, but ultimately ends in self-destruction and humiliation. Can also point to an unavoidable situation that is threatening, and the need for caution.

Reversed: Confusion, weakness, vulnerability. Regretful of past wrongs, sadness, mourning. Unfortunate turn of events that leads toward failure and ruin.

SIX OF SWORDS

Description: A helmeted man stands facing the gray mountains as he uses a winged staff to steer his small Viking-style boat toward the shore. The vessel's bow is in the form of a quail; the floorboard is pierced by six swords. He traverses the turbulent waters toward the calmer waters ahead. There is a break in the clouds on the horizon.

Meaning: Movement toward resolution of problem. Frustration and anxiety lessening; success. A smooth passage away from a troublesome situation, yet toward an unknown destination. A journey by water, or traveling.
Reversed: Unresolved frustration and anxiety. Stuck in a difficult situation that has no apparent solution. Delays, postponed project or journey.

SEVEN OF SWORDS

Description: A man has picked up five swords but neglects to pick up the two swords to his right, which indicates a careless approach to a task. He walks with his head down, looking to the ground rather than to the mountains ahead, as if fatigued or dispirited.

Meaning: Plans, hopes and great expectations counteracted by poor preparation, inadequate efforts and improper execution of tasks. Limited success, possibility of failure. Lack of conscience, misdirection, bad luck.
Reversed: Past errors interfere with success of project. Good potential for obtaining instruction, counseling, sound advice if sought.

EIGHT OF SWORDS

Description: A blindfolded woman, head bowed, stands passively with her arms bound to her sides by three circles of ropes tied to her midsection. Trapped in the forest of swords embedded in rock, which symbolize either her own or others' negative thinking, she is unable to see or move.

Meaning: Inability to free oneself from a difficult situation. Feeling bound and trapped by insecurity and fear. Mental distress caused by prior disappointment, failure and humiliation. Subject of criticism, slander, control and domination.
Reversed: Opposition, struggle, anxiety, but movement toward release from situation. Can refer to unexpected events, unforeseen tragedy.

NINE OF SWORDS

Description: A woman covers her face in her hands in despair as she leans over a casket-like object. Nine horizontal swords are suspended in the air while a maze of symbols extend as far as the eye can see behind her. Her hair is braided, and large crystal-like designs enclose the lower part of her bedclothes.

Meaning: Indecision, vacillation in an important matter, delay, failure. Disappointment, loss of self-esteem. Mental anguish, disturbing dreams, loneliness, despair, depression, desolation. Sometimes used to indicate ill health or loss through death.
Reversed: Uncertainty, doubt, mistrust, well-founded fear. Movement toward resolution, and the need for faith and time to heal.

TEN OF SWORDS

Description: A man lies prone on a slab of dry, cracked ground with ten swords embedded in his back along the spine, suggesting the death of his old way of thinking. He faces a barren mountain range in the distance. A cloth is draped over his lower body, exposing curved symbols rising from his belt. His right arm is covered by a crystal-like design.

Meaning: Trouble, sudden misfortune, defeat, ruin. Desolation, mental anguish, depression. Hitting bottom releases past influences, ends delusions and paves the way for a new life cycle. Does not represent violent death.

Reversed: The end of suffering, leading to a period of success. Can indicate a temporary advantage and a false sense of freedom from affliction.

PAGE OF SWORDS

Description: A Page, wearing a soft head covering, looks ahead as if at a distant object, or lost in his own thoughts. His right arm and shoulder are covered with a crystal-like design, and his large, unadorned sword stands ready beside him. Like his mind, which is active and inquiring but inexperienced, his sword is as yet not marked by his experience or his honors.

Meaning: A highly active young boy or girl who has an alert and inquiring mind, who may be willful and unkind in their search for power. Can indicate a person engaged in secret activities. The Page's presence suggests caution and defensiveness.

Reversed: A cunning and malicious youth who can cause great disturbance. Unforeseen problems, dangers or illness.

KNIGHT OF SWORDS

Description: A Knight holds a broad sword over his left shoulder. Near the hilt of the sword's blade is etched a simple design, a mark of the Knight's experience. His peaked helmet is decorated with a band of triangular shapes and is fastened by a thick chin strap woven from brown strips of material.

Meaning: An intelligent, clever, strong, young man of action. He can be overbearing, impetuous, determined to achieve his goals—even at the expense of others. Depending on surrounding cards, may indicate conflict and destruction.

Reversed: An arrogant, impulsive and self-centered young man who is excessive, impractical, incompetent. Strife, adversity, destruction.

QUEEN OF SWORDS

Description: A Queen, wearing a simple crown and a high-collared robe with a decorative accent on her throat chakra, faces forward. Her long brown hair flows freely, framing the highly ornate sword that crosses her chest, suggesting the defensiveness of her emotions. Five blooming roses cover the handle of the sword. Rows of curved symbols are on the bottom right corner of the card.

Meaning: A strong and independent woman who is highly intelligent, yet may be shrewd and unyielding in her dealings. A sad woman who is stern and cautious. Can represent poverty, barrenness, loss, separation, widowhood.
Reversed: A shallow-minded woman who is intolerant, domineering and vengeful. Can suggest spitefulness, malice, deceit.

KING OF SWORDS

Description: A King in a plumed helmet grips his sword as if ready for action. The base of the sword's blade is etched with black arches on both sides, suggesting his deep experience on the battlefield of life. The large opening in his metal helmet, at the crown chakra, indicates his receptivity to higher knowledge. On his sword arm is an imperial crown insignia, symbol of his authority.

Meaning: A brilliant man with a commanding air of authority, yet may be harsh and unfeeling in his judgements. Can portray a counselor, military commander, judge, politician. Represents sound advice, determination, productivity and caution.
Reversed: A brilliant, devious man ruthless in his quest for power and authority. Can warn of danger, perversity, brutality, or violence.

THE CUPS

ACE OF CUPS

Description: A single cup rests upon the surface of a pond surrounded by water lilies, which grow from their mud roots to blossom on the surface of the water. The goblet is decorated with triangular crystal structures, and a red sun rises from within the cup, filling the sky with rays of light.

Meaning: Abundance in all things, contentment, happiness, renewal, perfection, productivity. Fertility, birth, beginning of love relationship, renewal of self. Body-mind-spirit harmony, spiritual enlightenment, joy.

Reversed: False love, rejection, end of love relationship, overturning. Loneliness, despair, emotional instability, stagnation.

TWO OF CUPS

Description: A young couple face each other as they touch goblets in a toast. The man seems to be gazing into the distance while she looks directly into his eyes. His gloves have a tighter design than hers. An ornament covers his throat chakra. Her hair and robes form long, flowing patterns. She appears pregnant, suggesting they might be toasting the "fruit" of their union.

Meaning: Love, harmony, spiritual union, commitment, engagement, marriage. A deep friendship, meeting a kindred soul, respect and understanding. Cooperation, partnership, sharing good ideas in business.
Reversed: False love, lack of commitment, instability, misunderstanding. Disharmony, separation, divorce. Conflicts in friendship or business affairs.

THREE OF CUPS

Description: Three young women stand in front of an enormous yellow flower, seeming to rise behind them like a sun, blessing them. With up-raised cups held in their left hands, they toast each other. The central cup, the unifying symbol, is ornately designed, band upon band criss-crossing to the rim, as if to represent the steps taken to reach this happy outcome.

Meaning: Success and happiness, perfection, fulfillment, bountiful outcome, hopes realized. Solving a past problem brings comfort and healing, relief from anxiety. Merriment, joyous celebration of victory with a feast, good luck, good fortune.
Reversed: Overindulgence, gratification of sensual and sexual pleasures without love. Can relate to dismissing or hastily ending problems.

FOUR OF CUPS

Description: A youthful figure sits by a tree with his cloak pulled high to his face. He seems to be gazing off in space and does not focus on the three cups in front of him. A hand comes out of a cloud and offers him a fourth cup, yet it is ignored.

Meaning: Feeling unfulfilled, unhappy, weary, bored and unmotivated. Dissatisfaction with condition and direction of one's affairs. Longing for change, but unable to see or appreciate new opportunities. **Reversed:** New and possibly unusual opportunity, new relationship. Reawakening, rekindling of ambitions, new goals.

FIVE OF CUPS

Description: A dejected figure looks down at three spilled cups while two full cups stand behind him. His cloak is dull brown with crystal designs of the same color at the base of the garment. The tall marsh grass at the edge of the rise blows in the wind; seagulls circle in the sky.

Meaning: Feelings of sorrow, loneliness, dejection, guilt, or regret. Expectations unfulfilled; disappointment, frustration, possibly in relationship or inheritance. Focus is

upon the emptiness, rejection of life's pleasures, ignoring what one still has.
Reversed: Strength and hope renewed, new understanding, counting one's blessings. Return of friend or relation or a new alliance brings hope.

SIX OF CUPS

Description: A young boy and girl, wearing identical plain cloaks but individual hats, enjoy the fragrance of a bouquet of roses in a wooden cup. Below them five other cups contain a variety of floral arrangements, the central cup containing four lotus blossoms.

Meaning: Past influences favorably affect present life conditions. Creating a new atmosphere; forming new relationships; experiencing new learnings. Reflection and happy remembrance of the past. Meeting with old friend.
Reversed: Living in the past to escape present realities; loss of hope in future. Delays, stagnation. Fearing change; insecurity, immaturity.

SEVEN OF CUPS

Description: Seven cups set in a pyramid contain a variety of symbolic images: fruit and a butterfly; a cobra; a rainbow; a head rising upward; a blooming flower; a hand holding a tulip just beginning to open; and a helmet with lifelines to the sky.

Meaning: Indicates strong desires, active imagination, earnest seeking but scattered energies and unrealistic views cause difficulties. Problems in making decisions; attainment limited unless focus is on one goal and willpower is applied.

Reversed: Achievement of goals, realization of a project. Strong desire, clear sight, directed energy and determination bring success.

EIGHT OF CUPS

Description: A forlorn figure in a plain brown cape that appears to flow right into the earth leans on his walking stick at the water's edge. Bright pink cliffs to the left rising behind the gray land at the opposite shore suggest brighter days ahead. A waning crescent moon hangs in the empty sky.

Meaning: Retreat from an unpleasant situation, rejection, emotional withdrawal. Emotional isolation. Decline of a matter, which may lead the seeker to travel onward to more important things. Inner journey to discover higher aspects of existence.

Reversed: Entering and becoming entangled in an emotional situation. Celebration of earthly pleasures over spiritual pursuits.

NINE OF CUPS

Description: A robust, bearded man stands before a white triangular background above which nine cups are set on four levels. He wears an orange beret, suggesting the positive energy in his crown chakra. A red circle emphasizes his throat chakra, an area of great activity, such as eating, drinking, talking or laughing.

Meaning: Satisfaction, happiness, wishes come true. Accomplishment, success and assured future. Physical, emotional and spiritual well-being. Victory celebration, enjoyment of friends. May portray a happy, good-natured person who enjoys life.

Reversed: Intentions are good, but mistakes in plans and actions create problems. Can depict overindulgence in food, drink and merriment.

TEN OF CUPS

Description: A couple embrace as they look deeply into each other's eyes. A ring, adorned with a rose, secures her long ponytail. Ten cups are suspended in the air above the two figures, with a rainbow emerging from the largest, central cup. The illusion of a heart-shaped background is formed by the cups configuration overhead; a card of love.

Meaning: Completion, perfection, contentment, fulfillment and joy in love life. Happy family life, warm home, good friends, realization of the heart's desires. Success and security attained after experiencing many hard times in the past.

Reversed: Problems at home and in social life; lack of fulfillment, quarreling, frustration, anger and guilt. Can also indicate false love, infatuation.

PAGE OF CUPS

Description: A Page watches a fish rise out of a cup, suggesting the spiritual side of life emerging into consciousness. The figure's facial expression conveys sensitivity and introspection. The character's wide hat is topped with a spray of feathers and draped with a long red cloth. Two red tulips grow behind the figure.

Meaning: A warm, thoughtful young man or woman who may offer help. A quiet, sensitive and emotional boy or girl with creative talents beginning to develop. Can mean the beginning of a creative or business project, or the birth of a child.

Reversed: A charming and creative person who is immature and creates problems. Obstacles, deception, missed opportunity in creative or business project.

KNIGHT OF CUPS

Description: A young Knight with sensitive features rides with a cup before him, representing his holy grail, and a pair of tulips at his back. The visor is raised on his silver-winged helmet, offering a clear view ahead. His traveling cloak has a small shoulder patch on it.

Meaning: A creative and intelligent young man of vision who is confident and on the go. Can signify receiving an invitation or a proposition. The approach of an opportunity for a new beginning; arrival of an advancement.
Reversed: An untrustworthy person who has problems with emotions and excessive imagination. Also rivalry, deception, fraud.

QUEEN OF CUPS

Description: A beautiful Queen looks into the cup on her lap, as if seeking a vision. The cup, decorated at the rim, has a pink rose on the stem. The Queen's crown has high pointed peaks and a lavender jewel on the frontpiece above her third eye chakra. The drapings behind her crown create the illusion of lightning bolts.

Meaning: A generous woman who is kind and loving. She has a strong nature, is highly intuitive, and applies her clairvoyant talents practically. A warm, kind woman who is a devoted wife and mother. Can mean the enjoyment of love, a happy marriage, vision, success.

Reversed: A vain, overly emotional woman who may be well intended yet unreliable, or untrustworthy. Can indicate dishonesty or vices.

KING OF CUPS

Description: The King, sitting on his red throne set against an empty sky with jagged peaks in the background, grips an ornate cup with his right hand and his staff with his left, signifying the responsible and emotionally mature expression of his authority. A studded purple cap over a white skullcap is his crown and an amulet on a wide pink ribbon around his neck, his only jewel.

Meaning: A strong, responsible, dignified man who is an authority in art, science, law, or business. A kind, generous, intuitive man who offers sound advice. Can portray the successful application of strength and insight.

Reversed: A man who is dishonest and unyielding in his quest for power. Can indicate misuse of visions, injustice, loss, ruin.

THE PENTACLES

ACE OF PENTACLES

Description: A single red disc, embossed with a pentagram, is held aloft by a pair of gold flowers in full bloom and an ornate pattern of leaves. A solitary bud grows from one of the stems. The pale blue sky has puffs of white clouds, which typify this suit, providing the image of the physical world.

Meaning: The dawn of material and spiritual prosperity; wealth, comfort, elegance, happiness, well-being. Success in money matters, lucrative projects and investments, good fortune indicated. Can also stand for receiving a notification, document, degree.

Reversed: Improper attitude toward wealth; corruption, greed. False sense of security, failure in financial projects.

TWO OF PENTACLES

Description: A young juggler, wearing a simple outfit, stands before a turbulent sea. He is balancing a lemniscate containing two pentacles, while he concentrates on the one to his left. His hat is symbolic of the old juggler's cap, and the dark band on his forehead gives the appearance of a mask.

Meaning: Achievement of balance and harmony at a time of transition. Successful handling of complex situation of a dual nature, such as personal and business life. Suggests pleasure and gaiety, but future adjustments may be needed to overcome obstacles and turbulence.

Reversed: Inability to resolve opposing forces creates imbalance and loss of harmony within a situation. False sense of enjoyment.

THREE OF PENTACLES

Description: An apprentice, wearing a leather vest, is shown diligently working on carvings inside a church. Three pentacles are set into the top of the window above three columns. The youth's sleeves are rolled up, and he wears a red cap, similar to the pentacles in color and size.

Meaning: Knowledge and skill and the constructive use of creative talents. Mastering one's vocation; art, craft, skilled labor. Progressively gaining recognition and receiving material and spiritual reward. Can indicate maturity, confidence and security.

Reversed: Indifference to work situation, not using abilities to full potential. Immaturity, lacking direction, insecurity.

FOUR OF PENTACLES

Description: A young face is framed by a headband, long hair and a high-necked collar. A pentacle seems to rise out of the crown chakra, emphasizing the priority the youth places on material wealth and power as opposed to spiritual knowledge. A pentacle also covers the heart chakra, center of feeling, and both hands. Dark forms seem to encroach upon the figure from behind.

Meaning: Security and sense of identity based primarily upon having material possessions. Desire for wealth and its potential for power, possessiveness. Can express the ability to make a profit, or the possibility of a gift or inheritance.
Reversed: Insecurity caused by difficulties and delays in financial matters. Ambitions thwarted. Also, a possible loss of material possessions.

FIVE OF PENTACLES

Description: A forlorn couple walks past a church window that contains a design with five pentacles forming a cross. The woman carries a walking cane, indicating physical suffering, and wears a veil draped over her head. The man is dressed for cold weather and snow lays on the windowsill, attesting to the hostile environment.

Meaning: A time of troubles and strife regarding material concerns. Exhaustion of available funds, poverty. Portrays physical suffering, loneliness and spiritual destitution; and the need for refuge, comfort and spiritual guidance.
Reversed: Personal problems create discordant situations in your life. Extremely wasteful expenditures, excessive drinking, intemperate living. Turmoil, ruin.

SIX OF PENTACLES

Description: An elegantly clothed person sits at a table observing coins balancing on a scale. Four pentacles are set against the sky, and the remaining two are set on the table, indicating that spiritual values are applied to material life. The column, headdress and shirt trim are all pink, creating the illusion of a gently flowing stream from above; the spiritual flow through the crown chakra.

Meaning: A time of prosperity and comfort generously shared with others; philanthropy, humanitarianism. Success in business, the fair distribution of profits; receiving a bonus or gift. Indicates person who has a balanced material and spiritual life.
Reversed: Excessive desire for wealth; greediness, deception and envy. Mishandling of finances, unsound investments, debts.

SEVEN OF PENTACLES

Description: A young person stares intently at seven pentacles growing on a bush. The large center pentacle suggests the nearness of the harvest. The figure's cap, with its triangular design pointing toward the back of the crown chakra, is secured by a thick chinstrap. The gloved hand rests lightly on a goosehead cane, creating an image of petting a bird while waiting patiently.

Meaning: Success in money matters and financial rewards are forthcoming. Denotes ingenuity and hard work, and the success that it brings. Can indicate the need for making financial decisions and exercising patience and perseverance.

Reversed: Feeling alarm and anxiety in regard to money matters. Can point to impatience, lack of effort, or wasting time.

EIGHT OF PENTACLES

Description: A mustached man, wearing a studded leather cap and craftsman's apron, works in his shop. He is concentrating as he swings the wooden mallet; three small carving tools protrude from his pocket. Eight pentacles, of uniform size and shape, line the walls bordering the large window that is open to the sky.

Meaning: Successful employment of creative skills and craftsmanship in one's vocation, business, or commissioned work. Progress; movement toward completion of tasks at hand and the financial reward of finishing the project.
Reversed: Unambitious person toiling in drudgery, failure. Demanding excessive fees for poor quality work; or money loaned, extortion, greed.

NINE OF PENTACLES

Description: A woman stands in a vineyard holding a beautiful white peacock; they look eye to eye as if they are admiring each other. The bird has three pentacles along its long tail feathers; six pentacles decorate the woman's cape. The grapes have ripened on the vines and are waiting to be harvested.

Meaning: Success and financial security attained by foresight and the wise use of resources. Accomplishment, fulfillment. A sense of personal satisfaction and the freedom to enjoy the benefits of material independence.
Reversed: Entanglement in awkward situation. Be alert for deception, dishonesty, thievery. Poor judgement in financial matter, unwise investment, cancelled project.

TEN OF PENTACLES

Description: A couple with a small child stand at a gateway looking to the opulence and security of a castle set high upon a hill. The man's arm is around the woman, his cloak almost covering her. The child looks over his shoulder. Eight pentacles crown the archway. The remaining two form insignias above the piers, while two cultivated plants grow near their bases.

Meaning: Increased income, freedom from monetary concerns, a time of prosperity, acquiring material possessions, the security and enjoyment of home and family. Can indicate dignity and financial security from established family background, or inheritance.

Reversed: Problems in family life resulting from material loss—poor financial dealings, gambling, theft. Loss of dignity, reputation, or inheritance.

PAGE OF PENTACLES

Description: A Page stands against a blue sky with soft clouds. He stares intently at the large pentacle he is holding as if in contemplation. He wears a feathered beret secured by a plain chinstrap; a swath of material flows from the left side of the beret to the right shoulder, suggesting left brain dominance.

Meaning: A serious-minded and scholarly youth who represents diligence and hard work. A young person who is inquisitive and open to new ideas, but may be opinionated and critical. Can also indicate a messenger bringing news, information, advice.

Reversed: A self-indulgent and rebellious youth who represents intemperate living and wastefulness. Outside opposition, bad news.

KNIGHT OF PENTACLES

Description: An armor-clad Knight rides past rolling hills under a pale blue sky. The raised visor on his helmet provides a clear view of the path ahead. An orange plume fans out from its setting on the peak of his headgear. One pentacle forms an insignia on the shoulder piece, while the other emblazons the gorget, the protective throat piece.

Meaning: A hardworking and responsible young man of integrity and virtue, who represents the ability to serve with patience and efficiency. Also indicates setting material goals and working successfully toward their realization.

Reversed: A person who is passive, idle, lethargic. A time of rest, inactivity, stagnation. Can suggest discouragement and carelessness.

QUEEN OF PENTACLES

Description: A stately Queen gazes at the large pentacle that she holds on her lap. She is wrapped in an ermine robe trimmed in pink. Upon her head rests a winged headpiece that extends to her shoulders in the back. The band of her crown is decorated with peach and black semicircles.

Meaning: An intelligent and highly perceptive woman of distinction, who is devoted to her family and active in the community. An emancipated woman symbolizing wealth, independence, generosity and stateliness. Represents strength and material security.

Reversed: An insecure woman who is suspicious and conniving. Can indicate mischief, adversity, anxiety, fearfulness, misfortune.

KING OF PENTACLES

Description: A King gazes toward his left, while a pentacle looms in front of him. A yoked bull looks over his right shoulder, symbolizing the harnessed strength involved in the King's decision making. His imperial headdress is made of a soft material ringed with a crown on which are three red jewels, the largest one above the third eye chakra.

Meaning: An intelligent and mature man of valor and distinction, who is a considerate and affectionate partner. His skill, wisdom and ability to make decisions make him successful in business. He represents strong convictions, courage, talent, practicality and material success.

Reversed: A man who is corrupt, perverse, weak, unfaithful, materialistic. Caution against financial risks, danger of dishonesty.

CHAPTER SEVEN
INTUITION AND THE TAROT

The inclusion of intuitive information in a Tarot reading is the difference between a card reading and a Psychic Tarot Reading. The weaving of free associations, visions, intuitive thoughts, and other forms of insight can provide a tremendous boost to the Tarot reader's accuracy and ability to apply information from the cards to important moments in the seeker's life.

You can also learn to control and direct the flow of intuitive impressions in a Tarot reading through your intentions and your desires. You can intentionally steer into an area of the reading and gain greater understanding of a theme that you are interested in knowing more about. If your intentions are to gain deeper insight into a particular subject and you clear your mind to be an open receiver, then you are helping to direct the next series of impressions. Or, you can direct the reception by mentally asking your psychic self a question like, "I wonder why this is happening?" On a more emotional (body) level, if you want to know more about a particular subject and you remain open-minded and receptive, your desires will bring forth new information pertaining to that theme. If you reach a point in a Tarot reading where there is a lull in the reception of spontaneous psychic impressions, or you feel the need to shift your attention to a new subject, remember these tips.

This internal questioning may also prove to be beneficial as a more specific form of interaction with the cards in the spread. As you focus on the cards, you can ask questions such as, "Why is this disruption (the Tower) happening now, and what is the lesson being learned?" or "How will this new situation (Two of Cups) affect the seeker's job and home life?" If you are looking at a court card, you can inquire about the person being portrayed. You may ask, "What is this man (King of Swords, reversed) like emotionally, and how does he react to the seeker's plans to go back to college?"

If you are concentrating on a court card in one of the minor suits, which represents a person in the seeker's life, for example, you might see an actual vision of this person, or a symbolic image that characterizes him or her. A common occurrence is the reception of a symbolic picture that reveals part of the nature of the person in question; for example, seeing a man wearing a military officer's uniform when the person in question was never in the service. In this case, it is an image that describes the emotional side of him as a serious man who runs his life by rules and regulation and tries not to show his feelings.

The examples listed in this section are directly related to the Tarot cards to allow the student/reader to react spontaneously to their inspiring messages. They are the vehicle through which the psychic self relates the associated information to the conscious mind of the reader.

In the first example, the actual words of the divinatory meaning of the Six of Pentacles are used. The meaning is broken down into key phrases and followed by how I see the meaning visually delineated through the symbols contained in this card. This example should help the student understand the intuitive process used in choosing which aspect of the meaning pertains to a particular situation.

In the second example, details in the picture of the Tower are used to illustrate the application of information to a particular part of the seeker's life situation. I describe the places my eyes spontaneously land on when I first look at the card, and how I relate this to the area of application, be it home, business, or social life. Also shown are some instances of deeper meanings based on the images noticed at first glance.

In the third example, I use the Four of Swords to illustrate how intuition is stimulated by the imagery of the cards. These ideas, although outside the divinatory meanings, describe details of the work situation creating problems for the seeker.

Finally, I present "A Potpourri of Intuitions" from other cards, which came to me in relation to particular readings.

PLEASE NOTE: The insights into the particular cards shown should not be considered universal or absolute, but are to be used only to inspire your own system of interaction and insight.

SIX OF PENTACLES

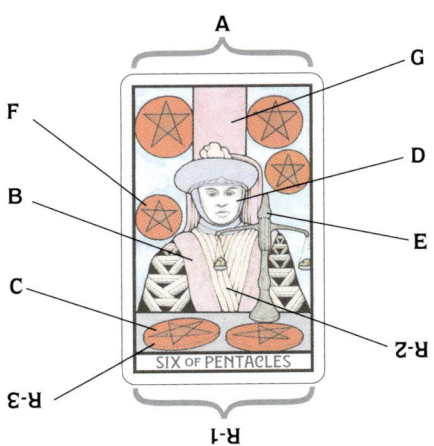

- **A A time of prosperity:** Overview of figure surrounded by six pentacles.
- **B and comfort:** Plush looking trim on garment.
- **C that is generously shared by others; philanthropy:** Two pentacles on table as offering to viewer of card.
- **D Humanitarianism:** Figure's facial expression seems to show deep thoughts of concern for humanity while looking at coins in pan balance.
- **E Success in business and the fair distribution of profits:** The weighing of the coins indicates shared profits.
- **F Receiving a bonus or gift:** Small pentacle over figure's right shoulder looks as if it has loosened from the other three and is coming down to the sitting figure.

G **Indicates person who has balanced material and spiritual concerns:** The pink column seems to be pouring into the hat and overflowing like a pink waterfall and becoming one with the trim of the garment. The pink trim acts as a border for the gentle folds of material that seem to funnel through the heart chakra and narrow down as they descend to the base chakra, or physical reality.

REVERSED

R-1 **Excessive desire for wealth; greediness:** The reversed picture looks like a divine hand has turned a can upside down to shake out its contents and have the person return to a more spiritual focus. Although the figure is upside down, the character holds onto the table from underneath, with eyes remaining transfixed upon the coins in the scale.

R-2 **Envy and deception:** The flow of pink energy is now originating from the physical chakra which lies "under the table," flows around the influence of the heart, and out of the bottom of the picture. The face gives no indication that something is wrong, as in a person lying while selling inferior goods, or a con artist covering up deception.

R-3 **Mishandling of finances, unsound investments, debts:** The general image of an upside-down financial picture. The large pentacles on the table seem to be ready to fall back up to join the other four, which are in the sky and out of sight. Even the smaller coins, or daily cash, will be lost.

THE TOWER

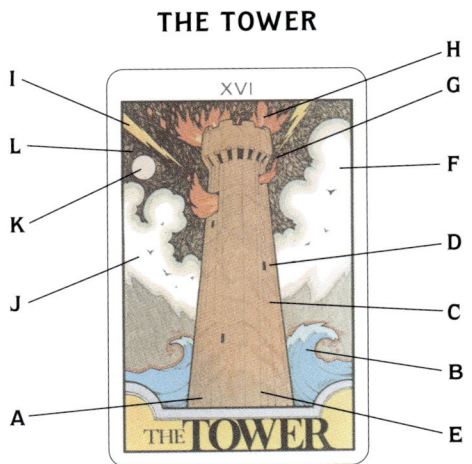

- **A** **Base of tower:** The base of the tower suggests problems in the home foundation and directs me to tune into how the relationship was begun and some of the unconscious contracts that were a part of its inception.
- **B** **Waves:** The crashing waves tell me that emotional turbulence is rocking the very foundation of the matter, and building in force.
- **C** **The rise of the tower:** When my eyes rest on the middle of the structure, it stands for problems centering in the areas of business or career.
- **D** **Windows:** When one of the tiny lower windows registers in my mind, I think about a person within the tower hiding in continued oppression.

E Composition of tower: Most times I see the tower as a brick structure. When the wood-grain pattern stands out, it reminds me of the story of the three pigs and the fragility of the house made of sticks.

F Clouds: The clouds represent major changes, and either seem to be closing in on the tower—OR moving away and clearing.

G Top of the tower: The structure's crown indicates problems in the seeker's way of thinking.

H Fire: The flames issuing from the windows seem to show a self-created fire (or problem).

I Lightning: The lightning bolts point to an outside influence creating, or contributing to, the disturbances, i.e., karma.

J Birds: The birds represent spiritual guidance either leaving OR returning (actually the seeker's state of being in touch with spiritual guidance). If they seem to be fleeing the storm in fright, it suggests the lack of insight to foresee the oncoming problem, and fleeing from changes in order to avoid the lessons they provide.

K Full moon: Noticing the moon brings my attention to the effect this difficult period has on the seeker's emotional life. At times the pink tint of the moon reveals a feminine influence in the matter.

L Sky: Sometimes the swirling patterns of the dark sky remind me of Vincent van Gogh and the mental turmoil that plagued the artist.

FOUR OF SWORDS

The following intuitions, although pertaining to the images on this card, were extracted from a Tarot reading that dealt with a woman's question about business. This was the first card in the Ancient Celtic Cross Spread ("This covers you"), and was surrounded by Pentacles and Cups in the layout.

A **Seeker inside suit of armor:** You go to work in your business clothes, or suit of armor, and try to hide both your femininity and your humanity. You also feel trapped in the "image" of a good corporate employee. You feel that you can't drop your defenses or you will be vulnerable. This also translates into your personal life in an opposite way whereby you set up an armor of toughness about you to remain unattached at this time in your life.

B **Three swords suspended above the armor:** There are three men at work who are putting tremendous pressure on you. The boss (B-1) mentally, a co-worker (B-2) psychically, and a subordinate (B-3) sexually. You feel you must hide—not move.

C **The horizontal sword:** There is a weapon that you have within your reach, but you are afraid to use it. It is your straightforwardness and toughness. You are afraid to reach for it because you may be leaving yourself open to the three men putting pressure on you.

D **The number four (and the suit of Swords):** You have a very practical and down-to-earth approach to your work and like to work systematically from the foundation up through mental calculations, yet you are a highly intuitive person who has the ability to work well with healing energies. This combination can make you feel tense at your work because you are repressing your deeper thoughts and insights as well as your sensitivity and desire to heal the problems of your fellow employees.

E **The clouds seem dark and ominous:** It feels like you are constantly looking out the windows at work and seeing the world as harsh and cruel. Like the Tin Man in *The Wizard of Oz*, you are afraid of (water/tears) emotions as if they could harm you if expressed. Also, if you let them loose, they would show the vulnerable side of you and your image would be lost forever.

F   **Pawn shop symbols:** At times your fear is that if you try to move, or reveal your true nature, you will be out of work and lose your possessions because you could not keep up the financial payments. The undue pressures of overextending yourself financially have you feeling at the mercy of your present employer, and by transference, of your immediate supervisor.

A POTPOURRI OF INTUITIONS

The intuitions of another teacher/reader, Holly Heintz, are marked with an asterisk, and are included for variety and added insight.

* **THE HIGH PRIESTESS:** The background scenery suggests loneliness and occasionally points to people in the seeker's life traveling while she remains behind. The red canopy sometimes suggests menstrual problems.

THE EMPEROR: The rams' heads on the sides of his throne show stubbornness and extreme obstinacy.

* **DEATH:** The sun gives the feeling of the seeker going to a hot climate.

* **THE DEVIL:** The Devil's red eyes can point to drunkenness, excessiveness, and lack of sleep.

* **THE SUN:** The extended V-shaped bar just below the word "Sun" looks like an open book, indicating a natural talent for creative writing, and potential for success in this field.

THREE OF RODS: Sometimes it looks like the sentry is peeking at the reader with a sideways glance, as if listening for danger. This can also suggest the seeker not trusting someone and keeping an eye on this person's behavior.

* **FOUR OF RODS:** Occasionally, the rods look like pens, which suggests the seeker has good writing ability.

* **SEVEN OF RODS:** The man appears frightened sometimes, relating to the seeker's feeling of not being up to the tasks ahead, and reassurance is in order.

* **NINE OF RODS:** The vertical rods occasionally look like jail bars in front of the figure, suggesting confinement either literally or figuratively.

TEN OF RODS: The white cloth hanging down from the figure's helmet looks like white hair, indicating an elderly person in the seeker's life who is overburdened and needing aid.

KNIGHT OF RODS: Looks like he is unwittingly leaving a trail of dark smoke issuing from the top of his head, suggesting anger and frustration creating problems for others. Occasionally refers to a person who has a "dark cloud" over his head that makes him tense, attracts negative situations, and blocks his spiritual energy.

THREE OF SWORDS: The three swords represent three relationships that cause sorrow and pain for the seeker. Focusing on each of the three handles gives me a sense of the three people and an understanding of the relationships. A few times it was three members in the seeker's family that were intuited.

* **KNIGHT OF SWORDS:** The knight's chinstrap looks like tree roots, showing the person to be rooted in a situa-

tion and doing what he feels he is supposed to do instead of what he wants to do.

* **FOUR OF CUPS:** The picture sometimes suggests the seeker about to receive a blow to the head from the cup overhead, which can be interpreted figuratively (an idea), or literally. In either case, paying attention is called for.

* **SEVEN OF CUPS:** A paradise for the imagination. The fruit of plenty leads to a man rising from below the surface or his emotions into the fresh air. A few times the hand holding the flower has appeared to be a singer holding a microphone, leading to a discussion about the seeker's singing talents. The helmet can indicate a pilot, motorcyclist, or a scuba diver.

TEN OF CUPS: In one reading I kept noticing the female figure's ponytail and spoke about how the seeker loved horses.

* **QUEEN OF CUPS:** The lightning bolts sometimes point to severe headaches being suffered by the seeker, or the person being portrayed by the card. The red throat decoration has suggested a sore throat, and when the queen's face looked puffy the card pointed to problems of weight gain and water retention.

KING OF CUPS: Occasionally, the King looks like a man staring into nothingness after excessive drinking—representing a person in the seeker's life doing the same.

* His scepter looks like a crutch (walking stick) which suggests limping, hip problems, needing a cane. His purple hand points to poor circulation.

TWO OF PENTACLES: The black space below the figure's

hat and his dissimilar eyes (where his right eye looks half closed and unfocused) indicate a problem in the seeker's thinking and perception caused by trying to handle opposing needs between his work and creative projects.

* At times this card relates to a person having two jobs; one part-time and one full-time.

   FOUR OF PENTACLES: The figure looks as if he can barely move or even breathe because of the oversized pentacles covering his hands, heart, and head—indicating the seeker's need to release his or her focus on money and relax more.

* **SEVEN OF PENTACLES:** When it looks like a Christmas tree full of ornaments, a message is given regarding that time of year as either a good or bad time; or having to wait until then for a desired event.

* **NINE OF PENTACLES:** Noticing the grapes suggested the seeker being wined and dined in a luxurious atmosphere. Once in a while it can feel more like a warning for the seeker to watch out for too much indulgence.

* **TEN OF PENTACLES:** The couple appear satisfied with their new home but the child tells me that they are going to find out otherwise soon enough. Also, the man's cape seems to be covering the female, suggesting he convinced her to move.

* **KING OF PENTACLES:** I frequently notice the King's face and describe a person in the seeker's life who is successful in business, but who is sad and lonely. When the bull stands out I speak about his false bravado and bullish nature as a defensive front for his insecurities.

CHAPTER EIGHT
PERFORMING PSYCHIC TAROT READINGS

The following is a suggested procedure that may help you to feel comfortable giving readings, whether it is for practice or as a service. It is not intended as a strict regimental method that must be followed in order to do the reading, but as an overview of the steps involved.

BEFORE THE READING

1. Prepare the room and the table for a pleasant and professional setting.
2. Spend a few minutes alone in the work area to relax, energize and connect in order to create the proper energy atmosphere.

> By working on your own personal healing you can consciously add healing energies to your Tarot readings. This involves establishing the healing energy within your own aura first and then allowing it to extend to the seeker's aura as well. Practice the self-healing technique described on page 55 and, when you are comfortable with it, make it a part of the preparation period before the reading.

3. Take out the Tarot deck, make sure the cards are clean, cut and shuffle them a few times, then set the pack on the table.

PERFORMING THE READING

1. Make the seeker comfortable, ask if he or she has any questions about the service you are providing or other concerns that need to be addressed before you begin.

2. Request that he not offer any information for the first ten minutes unless he does not understand what you are saying or feels the information is not valid. Explain that this is to keep your mind clear of mental calculations and open to intuitive information. Tell him that after the initial period you will welcome a dialogue and will work together as a team.

3. Explain the mixing and cutting procedure and hand him the deck (unless you are doing the mixing).

4. While the seeker is mixing the cards, spend a few minutes in quietude and go through the steps for relaxing, opening your energy, and connecting, to re-energize yourself and the room.

5. When he has completely shuffled the cards, instruct him to place the pack on the table and cut the cards into three piles to his left, using his left hand to do so.

6. Pick up the stacks so the cards to the seeker's right become the top cards. It's your choice whether to flip the cards up and over or sideways as you remove them from the stack; whichever way you choose, be consistent. Lay out the spread and begin speaking about what is revealed in the cards. The cards that are upside down to the reader are given reversed meanings.

7. As you are speaking about what is being revealed, allow for moments of interaction to help the seeker under-

stand the significance of what is being spoken about and to allay any fears or misunderstandings about the information you have given.

8. Afterward, provide an overview of the reading. Pay particular attention to information relating to problems and difficult situations and how one learns from them. Offer him your understanding and perspective on the reading to help him comprehend and work with the information after he leaves.

INFLUENCE OF DOMINANT CARDS IN A SPREAD

Three or more cards from a particular suit can be interpreted as to the influence the suit imparts. For example, four suit of Pentacles cards suggest the primary focus is on financial and material concerns, or that this area is a greater influence than the others.

Three or more court cards suggest the situation is strongly influenced by other people.

Two or more of a specific numbered card should be mentioned for their message. For example: three aces suggest many new beginnings and denote overall success.

Four or more major cards indicate a strong cosmic influence and imply that destiny is taking a hand in the matter in question.

The absence of a suit, or any major cards, shows an area not coming into play in regard to the question or issue not being focused on by the seeker.

THE YES/NO SPREAD

This quick and easy reading can be performed with only five cards. A yes or no question is concentrated upon while shuffling and cutting the deck as previously described. The Tarot cards are placed in a straight line in the order shown in the diagram below and indicate the strength of the yes (upright cards) or no (reversed cards) answer to the question. The cards are interpreted to explain the messages seen in them and to help the seeker understand the dynamics of the situation.

Card 1 Represents the **present situation** and indicates either a supportive or nonsupportive set of conditions in the present.

Card 2 Shows the influences in the **recent past**.

Card 3 Reveals the **immediate future**.

Card 4 Stands for the **distant past** and the **foundations of the matter**.

Card 5 Represents the **outcome or end result that will come in the future** (e.g., six months) if nothing is changed by the seeker.

Negative influences revealed through the meaning of the cards can be viewed as indicators pointing to possible changes that the seeker can put into effect. Other pertinent information is indicated by the presence of a majority of a suit, a number, Major Arcana cards, etc.

The following amount of upright cards lists the strength of the yes/no responses:

5 upright.....Definite YES; destined to be, smooth sailing
4 upright.....Most likely YES; minor problems to overcome
3 upright.....Possible YES, with changed plans and hard work
2 upright.....Possible NO; changes may not make it happen
1 upright.....Most likely NO; major problems block the way
0 upright.....Definite NO; destined not to be; problems may arise if plans are put into action

For more details regarding the reasons behind the answer, the next three cards from the deck can be added to the existing spread. (See diagram below.)

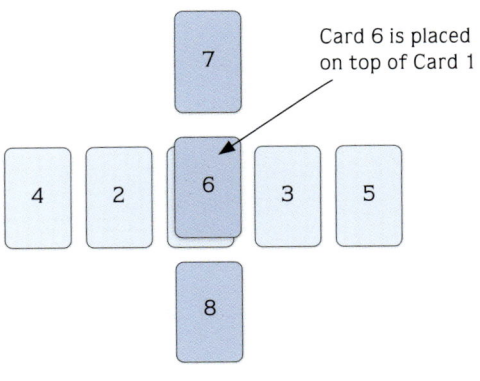

Each card represents the following:

Card 6 The mental influence from the seeker's conscious mind
Card 7 The higher self's message
Card 8 The subconscious patterns that influence the situation

THE ANCIENT CELTIC CROSS SPREAD
THE SIGNIFICATOR

The Significator is the central card in the spread, the center of the cross you will make with cards #1 through #6. Placed face up on the table, it becomes the symbolic image of the seeker within the context of the spread. Some readers choose the station of the court card according to the seeker's age as follows:

- Pages represent children and young boys or girls
- Knights stand for young men
- Queens portray women in all adult stages
- Kings portray mature men

After spreading out all four cards, e.g., the four Kings for a mature man, the reader asks the seeker to choose the card that fits his or her image of self, which will then become the symbolic representation of the seeker.

Other readers, myself included, do not generally use a Significator. I prefer to allow for the card that represents the seeker to come up somewhere in the spread, thus shedding light on how the seeker's personality and inner nature affect the situation being investigated.

THE ANCIENT CELTIC CROSS SPREAD

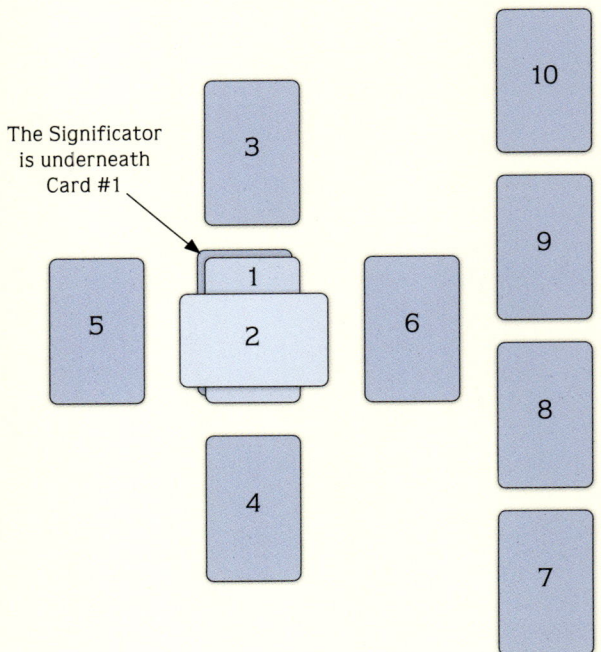

The Significator is underneath Card #1

1. This covers you.
2. This crosses you.
3. This crowns you.
4. This is beneath you.
5. This is behind you.
6. This is before you.
7. This represents you and your attitude toward the matter.
8. This is the effect of your environment.
9. This reveals your hopes and fears.
10. This is the outcome of the matter.

Another technique sometimes used is to ask the seeker to write down a question, which is placed face down or folded to hide the question, in the Significator's position, thus focusing the energies of the reading on the question the seeker wants to explore.

A Significator can also be a single card selected from a previous Celtic Cross spread. A common situation would be to use the tenth card—the position revealing the final outcome of the reading—as the Significator for a second Tarot reading. This is done when the card denoting the final outcome needs clarification, or the seeker requests further details regarding the meaning of the card. If the seeker places the card in the center of the table and concentrates on it while shuffling the cards, IT becomes the subject of the resulting spread.

MEANINGS ASSOCIATED WITH EACH POSITION

The bold faced words preceding the meaning of each position can be said aloud as each card is placed face up on the table.

1. **This covers you:** This card represents the general atmosphere pertaining to the question. It relates to the nature of the question, the general conditions and influences affecting the person and the situation, and the outside influences surrounding the question at hand.

2. **This crosses you:** This card crosses the first card to show the nature of the forces in opposition to the situation that are affecting it for good or evil. It can reveal the nature of the problems being experienced by the seeker or the positive forces that oppose the problems

as an aid. It can also reveal the way the seeker has reacted to these forces. This card is placed sideways but is always interpreted as if in an upright position.

3. **This crowns you:** This card reveals the hopes and aspirations of the seeker in relation to the question. It also represents the best achievement that can be expected under the present circumstances. It is also the message from the seeker's higher self in relation to the question asked.

4. **This is beneath you:** This card describes the foundation of the matter. This card explains what the seeker has already experienced in relation to the matter at hand. In most cases it points to a learning lesson, a constantly reoccurring theme in the seeker's life. (This card can also represent the subconscious view of the seeker regarding the matter.)

5. **This is behind you:** This card indicates a recent past influence, or one that is in the process of passing away. This influence should be evaluated in regard to the first two cards to determine its influence as a motivational force or its influence as a deterrent. If negative in nature: are the lessons it provided fully understood, or is it being invited back to complete the lesson?

6. **This is before you:** This card points to an upcoming situation and shows the influences that will be coming into action in the near future. It shows where the seeker is heading if no action is taken to alter the present situation. You can use this position to represent a specific future time, for example: six weeks, or three

months, and allow for psychic insight to reveal any variation in the time frame.

7. **This represents you and your attitude toward the matter:** This card reveals the seeker's position in the situation and his or her attitude toward the matter. (It represents the seeker's conscious view of it.) The person's inner nature and its effect on the situation may be seen most easily here.

8. **This is the effect of your environment:** The environmental factors will usually relate to the influence of family and friends. It can also describe the atmosphere in which the seeker lives, the workplace, the energy surrounding the seeker, and his or her position in life.

9. **This reveals your hopes and fears:** This card indicates the hopes and fears of the seeker concerning the matter. It can reveal hopes through a positive meaning, fears through a negative meaning. It can also indicate fear of seemingly positive influences such as intimacy, personal authority, or even success.

10. **This is the outcome of the matter:** The tenth card represents the potential future resulting from the circumstances revealed by the nine cards preceding it. This card can be assigned a specific time frame (e.g., twelve weeks or six months) as was done with the sixth card. It is important to work intuitively with this card to provide understanding and practical insight to the seeker regarding its message. If the tenth card does not offer a clear understanding of the outcome,

or no clear conclusions can be drawn from it, this card can be used as the Significator for a second reading, which can provide more detailed information regarding the outcome of the matter.

AUTHOR'S VIEW OF CELTIC CROSS SPREAD

The Significator

The Significator portrays the seeker's personality and present state of development as a person. It represents the way the seeker sees self and how others perceive him or her to be.

The Lesser Cross

The small cross formed by cards #1 and #2 stands for the present life situation being experienced by the seeker. This usually describes the mundane aspects of the seeker's present conditions and reveals the question being asked in the Tarot reading.

The Greater Cross

The vertical line of the greater cross, formed by cards #3 and #4, represents the nonphysical influences flowing down to the seeker. The uppermost card (#3) is the energy and the message offered to the seeker from his or her higher self. The bottom of the cross (card #4) is the way this influence is experienced by the seeker's subconscious mind and the working through of karmic learning lessons on an unconscious level.

The horizontal beam of the greater cross, formed by cards #5 and #6, describes how the seeker translates these influences into daily life. The card to the left (#5) describes the lesson being released, and the card to the right (#6) the upcoming lesson being prepared for. These influences refer to the way one grows as a human being by experiencing both positive and negative life situations and developing a deeper understanding of self and life.

The Vertical Ladder

The four cards to the right of the cross, numbers seven through ten, symbolize the pathway the seeker is walking toward the future.

The bottommost card (#7) shows the starting point in the working out of the situation shown in the preceding cards. It reveals the seeker's present beliefs and attitudes, which can help the seeker realign these factors to facilitate the learnings revealed in the reading.

The environmental influences (card #8) describes how the seeker is influenced by the people and life situations he or she is encountering. Positive influences can be embraced for promoting growth. By understanding the negative influences, the seeker can accept aid offered for dealing with them.

The card of hopes and fears (#9) reveals how the seeker is affected by his or her views of both self and life situations in regard to risk-taking and inhibitions. The fears indicate apprehensions, anxieties, dread and hesitations. The hopes indicate desires, expectations, enthusiasm, assurances and faith. In some instances the seeker can be afraid of success or accomplishments based on unconscious fears.

The uppermost card (#10) expresses the final outcome of the reading and shows the rewards and learning lessons being offered in the near future. It represents the culmination of the influences shown in all of the previous cards and reveals the development achieved as the result of the situations shown in the reading. An analogy is in the painting of a house: it is the work accomplished in the present placement of the ladder, before moving the ladder to the next position alongside the house.

AN EXAMPLE OF
TENTH CARD INTERPRETATION AND INSIGHT

An upright Nine of Swords was the subject of a lengthy discussion at the end of a Tarot reading I gave recently. After explaining the negative meaning of the card as the eventual outcome, I tied the information from the other nine cards together to provide an overview of the situation. I then proceeded to add on pertinent information to help the seeker work with the negativity, to accept the card instead of turning away from it, and to work toward making decisions that would help him to work it through.

- He was being forewarned of a situation that could be prepared for and dealt with. If it was not entirely avoidable then he might be able to buffer its effects and minimize its disturbance on his consciousness and his loved ones. In the least it could provide for a period of rest, vacation, soul-searching, or working on a personal project. I sensed his desire to be a writer and spoke at length about how this type of period can be used to inspire his creative writing and to act in a therapeutic way to release his feelings through writing them into the story.

- Life is composed of cycles that flow like rolling hills. We tend to enjoy walking or riding downhill and begrudgingly climb up the next. In other instances we are troubled by downhill curves on our financial graphs. In other words, expect the ups and downs in life, remain balanced during all phases, and measure your total progress.
- We learn and grow from the difficult times and trials we go through. If we look into our past honestly, we find tremendous positive changes resulting from going through troublesome times. An analogy of putting metal into the fire and hammering it into a tool or a weapon was given.
- I explained the effects of the past were symbolized by the crystal patterns on the garment and therefore could be worked through, symbolized by the removal of the garment.
- The futuristic symbols appeared to be a winding maze of razor-sharp obstacles, and a pathway through them was possible, although a few nicks and scratches could be expected.
- The woman appeared to be covering her face as if afraid of a bad dream, and she seemed to be avoiding looking ahead toward her future. She couldn't "face" the issues in her life; therefore an acceptance of the influence was suggested, using the analogy that keeping one's eye on an object heading in one's general direction is a good way to avoid being hit by it full force. Sensing that baseball was important to him, I used the analogy of keeping "his eye on the ball" to

know how to react to it to support this view. I also saw an image of a bullfight in my mind and related the way the matador directs the charging bull away from his body through close observation and the movement of the cape.
- Having also sensed self-delusion and insecurity as factors, I reminded him of the need to see things in clearer focus and be able to experience momentary losses without feeling himself to be defeated and evaluating himself as a total failure.

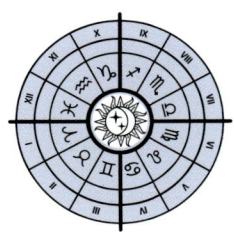

THE ASTROLOGICAL SPREAD

After shuffling and cutting the deck, place one card in each of the twelve positions shown on page 175 in a counterclockwise fashion. Each position represents the following:

1. **PERSONALITY:** How you relate to life, and present yourself to the world. Attitudes.
2. **FINANCIAL MATTERS:** Material values and possessions, your livelihood and ability to make and handle money.
3. **MIND & TRAVEL:** Your conscious mind, ability to apply intelligence, communication, siblings, short journeys.

4. **HOME LIFE:** Your childhood foundations, family relations, your home and your life directions, real estate.
5. **EMOTIONS & ROMANCE:** Your romantic views, your love life, children, your emotional nature, creativity, pleasures.
6. **HEALTH & WORK:** Unconscious influences, your health, how you apply yourself to work, service, responsibilities.
7. **MARRIAGE & PARTNERSHIPS:** Your ability to relate to others intimately, your circle of partners, friends, and enemies, business associates.
8. **LIFE & INFLUENCES:** Occult matters, hidden influences in your life, how others relate to you, sexuality, psychic abilities.
9. **SPIRITUALITY & JOURNEYS:** Your higher mind, philosophy and religion, mystical states of mind, and long journeys.
10. **PROFESSION & AMBITIONS:** Your professional status and goals, business and public life, and your sense of self-value.
11. **HUMAN RELATIONS:** Your ability to socialize and work with groups, humanitarian efforts, outside forces. Also hopes, fears, and aspirations.
12. **LIMITATIONS, KARMA:** Your hidden personality, strengths and weaknesses, the limitations imposed upon you, karma and the working out of your destiny.

For a more in-depth reading, place two more cards in each position by repeating the circular placement two more times.

The Influences of the Twelve Houses

CIRCULAR SPREAD FOR YEARLY FORECAST

Instead of using astrological houses for the twelve positions, the same pattern can be used to map out the upcoming year by designating each of the twelve positions to represent a month. The three cards in each position are interpreted as the message for that month and viewed in relation to the whole picture.

APPENDIX

NUMEROLOGICAL CORRELATION TO THE TAROT

Numerology is the study and expression of the occult meaning of numbers and their application to personality traits and life situations. The Greek philosopher Pythagoras (ca. 572-497 BC) proposed that numbers were the secret keys to the universe. Through the ages, occultists have analyzed and interpreted the vibratory condition of the universe through the study of numbers. Their formulas and equations have been reduced to reveal the essence of each number and the degree of harmony in their interaction.

Practical numerology is the conversion of the letters of the alphabet to single digit numbers and the interpretation of names and dates by reduction to vital numbers, for example,

- A = 1, B = 2, C = 3 ... H = 8, I = 9, J = 10, etc.
- J = 10 = 1 + 0 = 1, K = 11 = 1 + 1 = 2, L = 12 = 1 + 2 = 3, etc.

A birthdate of 08/08/1952 = 8 + 8 + 1 + 9 + 5 + 2 = 33 = 6.

Numerology was a contributing factor in the derivation of the divinatory meaning of the Tarot cards. The numerological meaning of each number is briefly described below.

ZERO: Unrestricted, unlimited potential, absolute, omnipresence, infinity. Pure spirit, unmanifested ideas, creative energy that has not been applied to the physical world. Nothingness.

ONE: Beginnings, initiating something new, the first. Primary, the essence, the active principle, originality. Sense of self, ego, "I AM," decisiveness, willpower, courage, persistence, dynamic energy. A daring person with a constructive mind, a pioneering spirit, and leadership qualities who appears to be self-sufficient.

TWO: Duality, polarity, alternate choices, vacillation, fluctuating situations, opposition, antagonism, conflicts. Balance. Seeking compromise, momentary peace and tranquility from opposing ideas and desires, reflection and meditation. An affectionate, enthusiastic, and highly sensitive person who is gentle, considerate, and needs companionship.

THREE: Trinity, joining of opposing forces creates a third force and brings harmony, childbirth. Careful planning, care to details, orderly growth, expansion, improvement, spiritualization. The expression and practical application of artistic talents and intuitions. A joyful, spontaneous, and outgoing person who is charismatic, devoted, compassionate, generous, collaborative.

FOUR: Solid foundations, stable situations, security, materiality, substantiality, tradition. Methodical planning and building upon foundations, cautionary measures, tangible accomplishments. A pragmatic and down-to-earth person who is inventive, ambitious, hard-working, and shows patience and perseverance.

FIVE: Freedom, independence, travel, communication. Mind, intellect, scientific logic, creativity, adaptability. Difficult situations, problems dealing with people and relationships, arguments, struggles, strife, need to change and adapt. A clever, versatile, and highly active person who is impatient, excitable, changeable, and easily discouraged.

SIX: Love, self-sacrifice, loyalty. Equilibrium, balance of opposites, adaptation, cooperation, accomplishment, contentment, assurance, success. Duties, obligations, responsibilities. A person with a dual nature who is loving and loyal to family and friends, sensitive, and appreciates the fine arts, yet can be lazy and indiscreet.

SEVEN: Success, completion of tasks, mastery, triumph. A period of rest and reflection, introspection, temporary repose. Insight, wisdom, mystical and spiritual attainment. A caring and understanding person who is intelligent, highly creative, and a deep thinker. A person who is a good friend and appreciates the finer things in life.

EIGHT: Authority, responsibility, strength, will, discipline, fortitude. Power, intensity, money. Ability to transmute energy and see on many levels. Cycles, alternating currents, opposing forces, change. An honest, sincere, intelligent, and outspoken individual who correctly applies willpower in a practical yet progressive manner.

NINE: Completion, endings, accomplishment, reaching one's goals, skill, and competence. Attainment of higher consciousness, understanding, wisdom. Compassion, humanitarianism, altruism, search for truth. A gentle, romantic, and sympathetic person who is imaginative and artistically talented.

TEN: Manifestation of the zero, and the higher octave of number one (10 = 1 + 0 = 1), empowers the qualities of one. Rebirth.

ELEVEN: Intuition, ability to receive from higher source, mysticism, spirituality. A higher octave of two (11 = 1 + 1 = 2) that is idealistic, excitable, changeable, sometimes unstable.

TWENTY-TWO: Mastery over the physical universe, the higher octave of four (22 = 2 + 2 = 4). Master builder, one who applies knowledge and insight to the physical plane. An uplifting new age builder who works with groups.

ASTROLOGICAL CORRELATION TO THE MAJOR ARCANA

The following lists each Major Arcana card alongside the general meaning of the astrological sign or planet associated with it.

0. **THE FOOL = The Planet Uranus:** Instigates sudden unpredictable change, revolution, transmutation. Rebellion, freedom, independence. Impulsive, high-spirited, eccentric.

I. **THE MAGICIAN = The Planet Mercury:** Intellect, reason, logic, adaptability, communication, skill. Intuition, meditation, receiving from above and communication through the conscious mind.

2. **THE HIGH PRIESTESS = The Moon:** The feminine principle, understanding, adaptation, assimilation, feelings, emotions, moods. Instinct, the psyche, subconscious, receptivity, memory, the past.
3. **THE EMPRESS = The Planet Venus:** Love, creativity, art, fertility, harmony, balance. Comfort, luxury, grace, beauty, charm.
4. **THE EMPEROR = Aries, the Ram:** Pioneering, initiative, authoritative, straightforwardness, impatience, impulsiveness, determination, qualities of leadership. Rules the brain, translating ideas into actions.
5. **THE HIEROPHANT = Taurus, the Bull:** Stability, reliability, conviction, tradition, stubbornness, inertia. Money, material possessions, physical structuring of the universe. Rules the ears and throat, listening to and expressing the inner voice.
6. **THE LOVERS = Gemini, the Twins:** Duality, changeable opinions, choosing between the mind and the emotions. Love of home and family relationships. Logic and scientific reasoning, self-improvement, short-term travel.
7. **THE CHARIOT = Cancer, the Crab:** Sensitivity, protection, surrounding self with defenses. Psychic. Effort to maintain emotional equilibrium and inner harmony. Triumph over emotions through the challenge of relationships, family, nurturing.
8. **STRENGTH = Leo, the Lion**: Strength, dynamic energy, intensity, courage, loyalty, nobility. Authority, warmth, love, affection, romance. Self-centeredness, pomposity, dramatic, self-expression, creativity, success.

9. **THE HERMIT = Virgo, the Virgin:** Detail-oriented, technique, usefulness, mental discrimination, analytical faculties. Perfectionist, critical, cautious, orderly, conscientious, teaches by example, devoted to humanitarian service.

10. **THE WHEEL OF FORTUNE = The Planet Jupiter:** Opportunity, growth, expansion, success, fortune, generosity. Harmony, high aspirations, fulfillment, happiness, joviality. Wisdom, religion, law.

11. **JUSTICE = Libra, the Balanced Scales:** Balance, harmony, peace, grace, love, sympathy, fairness, tact, diplomacy, equality, justice. Courtesy, artistic sense, need for decisiveness. Partnerships.

12. **THE HANGED MAN = The Planet Neptune:** Self-sacrifice, idealism, receptivity, mysticism, spirituality. Impressionability, imagination, illusion, delusion, self-deception.

13. **DEATH = Scorpio, the Scorpion/Eagle:** Change, transmutation, regeneration, death and rebirth, emotional intensity, power, sexuality, magic. Secrecy, suspicion, revenge, deep emotions, unconscious motivation, psychoanalysis.

14. **TEMPERANCE = Sagittarius, the Archer:** The teacher, higher self, religion, application of spirituality. Truth, honesty, candidness, enthusiasm, receptivity, tolerance, sincerity, good judgement, benevolence, generosity, beauty, long-distance travel.

15. **THE DEVIL = Capricorn, the Goat:** Materiality, judgement, condemnation, domination, ambition, industry,

patience, dignity. Worldliness, outer recognition of success. Karma, restriction, limitation, discouragement.

16. **THE TOWER = The Planet Mars:** Energy, erratic action, abrupt change, excessive force, anger, irritation, war, sexual energy, penetration. Initiates actions, self-assertiveness, determination, courage.

17. **THE STAR = Aquarius, the Water Bearer:** Inspiration, insight, knowledge, intuition. Hopes, wishes, idealism, sympathy, friends, group consciousness, humanitarianism. Patience, perseverance, progressiveness, originality, independence.

18. **THE MOON = Pisces, the Fish:** Dreams, imagination, introspection, psychic, mystical, occult, secretiveness, solitude. Ambition, creativity, sympathy and kindness. Confusion, insecurity, sensitivity, gullibility.

19. **THE SUN = The Sun:** Love, joy, happiness, success, recognition. Power, vitality, activity, determination, will, authority, sense of self, spirit.

20. **JUDGEMENT = The Planet Pluto:** Intensity, upheavals, transmutation, transformation, destruction and rebirth, healing. Higher forces, hidden power. The masses, compulsive behavior, fanaticism.

21. **THE WORLD = The Planet Saturn:** Discipline, concentration, structuring, stabilization. Inhibition, karma, duty, responsibility, steadiness, perseverance. Striving for attainment of prosperity and recognition.

TRENDS IN THE TAROT CARDS

The following charts summarize the meaning of each Tarot card as being either positive, negative, or mixed, in both the upright and reversed positions. It is designed to help students understand the general trends in each suit and in the Major Arcana.

LEGEND	
+	positive
−	negative
+/−	mixed
(+)	mostly positive
(−)	mostly negative

THE MINOR ARCANA

RODS		
#	UPRIGHT	REVERSE
1	+	−
2	+/−	(−)
3	+	+/−
4	+	(+)
5	(−)	(+)
6	+	−
7	+	−
8	+	−
9	+	−
10	(−)	−
P	+	−
Kn	+	−
Q	+	−
K	+	(−)

SWORDS		
#	UPRIGHT	REVERSE
1	(+)	−
2	−	(−)
3	−	−
4	(+)	−
5	−	−
6	(+)	−
7	−	(−)
8	−	(−)
9	−	(−)
10	−	(+)
P	+/−	−
Kn	+/−	−
Q	+/−	−
K	+/−	−

CUPS		
#	UPRIGHT	REVERSE
1	+	−
2	+	−
3	+	−
4	−	+
5	−	+
6	+	−
7	(−)	+
8	(+)	−
9	+	−
10	+	−
P	+	−
Kn	+	−
Q	+	−
K	+	−

PENTACLES		
#	UPRIGHT	REVERSE
1	+	−
2	(+)	−
3	+	−
4	(+)	−
5	−	−
6	+	−
7	+	−
8	+	−
9	+	−
10	+	−
P	+	−
Kn	+	−
Q	+	−
K	+	−

THE MAJOR ARCANA			
#		UPRIGHT	REVERSE
1	The Magician	+	−
2	The High Priestess	+	−
3	The Empress	+	−
4	The Emperor	+	−
5	The Hierophant	+	−
6	The Lovers	+	−
7	The Chariot	+	−
8	Strength	+	−
9	The Hermit	(+)	−

THE MAJOR ARCANA, continued			
#		UPRIGHT	REVERSE
10	The Wheel of Fortune	+	−
11	Justice	+	−
12	The Hanged Man	+	−
13	Death	(−)	−
14	Temperance	+	−
15	The Devil	−	(+)
16	The Tower	−	(−)
17	The Star	+	−
18	The Moon	−	+
19	The Sun	+	(−)
20	Judgement	+	−
21	The World	+	−
0	The Fool	(+)	−
0/22	The Fool	+	−

BIBLIOGRAPHY

BENNETT, SIDNEY
Tarot for the Millions, Los Angeles, CA: Sherbourne Press, Inc., 1967

BUNKER, DUSTY
Numerology and Your Future, Gloucester, MA: Para Research, 1980

CASE, PAUL FOSTER
The Tarot, Richmond, VA: Macoy Publishing Co., 1947

CIRLOT, J.E.
A Dictionary of Symbols, New York: Philosophical Library, Inc., 1962

CONNOLLY, EILEEN
Tarot: A New Handbook for the Apprentice, North Hollywood, CA: Newcastle Publishing Company, Inc., 1979

DOUGLAS, ALFRED
The Tarot, New York: Penguin Books, 1973

GERULSKIS-ESTES, SUSAN
The Book of Tarot, Stamford, CT: U.S. Games Systems, Inc., 1981

GRAVES, F. D.
The Windows of Tarot, Dobbs Ferry, NY: Morgan & Morgan, Inc., 1973

GRAY, EDEN
The Tarot Revealed, New York: New American Library, 1969

HALL, MANLY P.
The Secret Teachings of All Ages, Los Angeles, CA: The Philosophical Research Society, Inc., 1977

JUNJULAS, CRAIG
Self Discovery Through Psychic Awareness, Yonkers, NY: 1982

KAPLAN, STUART R.
The Encyclopedia of Tarot, Stamford, CT: U.S. Games Systems, Inc., 3 volumes, 1978, 1986 and 1990.

MARCH, MARION & McEVERS, JOAN
The Only Way To Learn Astrology, San Diego, CA: Astro Computing Services, 1980

WAITE, ARTHUR E.
The Pictorial Key to the Tarot, Stamford, CT: U.S. Games Systems, Inc., 1983

ZAIN, C. C.
The Sacred Tarot, Los Angeles, CA: The Church of Light, 1969

ZOLAR
The Encyclopedia of Ancient and Forbidden Knowledge, New York: Nash Publishing, 1970

ABOUT THE AUTHOR

Craig Junjulas is a metaphysical teacher, clairvoyant, author and lecturer who lives in Sedona, Arizona. He is a psychic consultant, hypnotherapist, and spiritual counselor who offers private sessions and teaches classes across the country.

As a public speaker, he has been a presenter for over 40 years for metaphysical centers, private groups, continuing education programs, conferences, hypnotherapy conventions, and more. He was the former director of the Foundation for Psychic Development and is the founder of the Sedona Metaphysical Spiritual Association.

As a teacher, Craig helps his students to help themselves by stimulating their own higher natures, thus leading naturally to higher self-discovery. He recognizes that the greater purpose of expanding the mind is to open the heart and apply this increased awareness to helping others in need.

NOTES
PERSONAL INTERPRETATIONS & INTUITIONS
THE MAJOR ARCANA

0. THE FOOL _____
_____
_____

1. THE MAGICIAN _____
_____
_____

2. THE HIGH PRIESTESS _____
_____
_____

3. THE EMPRESS _____
_____
_____

4. THE EMPEROR _____
_____
_____

5. THE HIEROPHANT _____
_____
_____

6. THE LOVERS _____
_____
_____

7. THE CHARIOT _____

8. STRENGTH _____

9. THE HERMIT _____

10. THE WHEEL OF FORTUNE_____

11. JUSTICE _____

12. THE HANGED MAN _____

13. DEATH _____

14. TEMPERANCE_____

15. THE DEVIL _____
_____
_____

16. THE TOWER _____
_____
_____

17. THE STAR_____
_____
_____

18. THE MOON_____
_____
_____

19. THE SUN _____
_____
_____

20. JUDGEMENT_____
_____
_____

21. THE WORLD_____
_____
_____

THE MINOR ARCANA
SUIT OF RODS

ACE _____
_____
_____

TWO _____
_____
_____

THREE _____
_____
_____

FOUR _____
_____
_____

FIVE _____
_____
_____

SIX _____
_____
_____

SEVEN _____
_____
_____

EIGHT _____
_____

NINE _____
_____

TEN _____
_____

PAGE _____
_____

KNIGHT_____
_____

QUEEN _____
_____

KING _____
_____

SUIT OF SWORDS

ACE _____
_____
_____

TWO _____
_____
_____

THREE _____
_____
_____

FOUR _____
_____
_____

FIVE _____
_____
_____

SIX _____
_____
_____

SEVEN _____
_____
_____

EIGHT _____
_____
_____

NINE _____
_____
_____

TEN _____
_____
_____

PAGE _____
_____
_____

KNIGHT_____
_____
_____

QUEEN _____
_____
_____

KING _____
_____
_____

SUIT OF CUPS

ACE _____
_____
_____

TWO _____
_____
_____

THREE _____
_____
_____

FOUR _____
_____
_____

FIVE _____
_____
_____

SIX _____
_____
_____

SEVEN _____
_____
_____

EIGHT _____
_____
_____

NINE _____
_____
_____

TEN _____
_____
_____

PAGE _____
_____
_____

KNIGHT_____
_____
_____

QUEEN _____
_____
_____

KING _____
_____
_____

SUIT OF PENTACLES

ACE _____
_____
_____

TWO _____
_____
_____

THREE _____
_____
_____

FOUR_____
_____
_____

FIVE _____
_____
_____

SIX_____
_____
_____

SEVEN _____
_____
_____

EIGHT _____
_____
_____

NINE _____
_____
_____

TEN _____
_____
_____

PAGE _____
_____
_____

KNIGHT_____
_____
_____

QUEEN _____
_____
_____

KING _____
_____
_____

For our complete line of tarot decks, books, meditation and yoga cards, oracle sets, and other inspirational products, please visit our website:

www.usgamesinc.com

Follow us on:

U.S. GAMES SYSTEMS, INC.
179 Ludlow Street
Stamford, CT 06902 USA
Phone: 203-353-8400
Order Desk: 800-544-2637
FAX: 203-353-8431